A SUSSEX GUIDE

SALACIOUS SUSSEX

VIV CROOT

INTRODUCED BY
SIMON FANSHAWE

Illustrated by
Curtis Tappenden

SNAKE RIVER PRESS

SNAKE RIVER PRESS

Book No 15
Books about Sussex for the enthusiast

Published in 2009 by
SNAKE RIVER PRESS
South Downs Way, Alfriston, Sussex BN26 5XW
www.snakeriverpress.co.uk

ISBN 978-1-906022-14-3

This book was conceived, designed and produced by
SNAKE RIVER PRESS

Additional text by Ann Kramer and Marcus Weeks
Illustration © Curtis Tappenden

ART DIRECTOR & PUBLISHER *Peter Bridgewater*
EDITORIAL DIRECTOR *Viv Croot*
EDITOR *Rob Yarham*
PAGE MAKEUP *Richard Constable & Chris Morris*
ILLUSTRATOR *Curtis Tappenden*
CONSULTANT *Lorraine Harrison*

This book is typeset in Perpetua & Gill Sans,
two fonts designed by Eric Gill

Printed and bound in China

DEDICATION

For PB and his patience

CONTENTS

FOREWORD

I have just read this book in one sitting and I feel deliciously and guiltily, unclean. A parade of murderers, smugglers, adulterers and con men have danced off the page. Most of them dregs, ruiners of other lives. And yet we love them. Why? These men and women driven to break the bargain we have with each other to live in peace and trust. It's because they fascinate. They live just a very few inches away, certainly no more than six, from our own fears of our own very worst deeds.

Reading about these characters is like watching a ventriloquist's dummy insult the audience. As the dummy breaks every social convention of politeness, we of course identify with the puppeteer, who through the dummy has bought permission to go everywhere we would not dare. It's thrilling to watch. Just as reading of murder, revenge and terrible violence gives us a vicarious thrill while reminding us of the line we know we must not cross. Sybil Thorndike was once asked, after 60 years of marriage, whether she'd contemplate divorce. She said 'Divorce? Never. Murder, yes, but never divorce'. We all know what she meant.

So herein you will find the adulterous secrets of the man who founded the modern political party; the degenerate who sculpted his own genitals in marble while training to be a monk; the judge who tried his own would-be murderer; the men whose love and jealousy led them to poison each other with arsenic; men and women who chopped up, stabbed, walloped with hammers, dissolved in acid and poisoned with pie or chocolate their lovers and spouses and even some strangers. There are smugglers far more violent than any modern Mafia don could hope for and political fraudsters who make Jeffrey Archer look saintly. And, of course, the Bloomsberries.

And it all happened in Sussex. It turns out it isn't just murdered women who are locked away in trucks till their remains demand to be discovered. It is the long-hidden salacious secrets of this county that are disinterred by this precocious book that brazenly says of itself 'we are here for the filth'!

SIMON FANSHAWE

INTRODUCTION

'It is a sin to believe evil of others, but it is seldom a mistake.'

H.L. MENCKEN

People have pointed out to me that salacious strictly means lecherous or sexually wanton (from the Latin *salire*, to jump, don't you know), and that as I have not confined myself entirely to lustful activity, it is not really correct, from an etymological angle. They say I should have gone for saucy or seditious or scurrilous or scandalous, or anything else that combines dubious activities with geography in a pleasing alliteration based on the letter s. However, this is a Humpty Dumpty post-modern world in which words can mean what you want them to, so I have decided to go with salacious, because I like the sound and it has overtones of saltiness (from a completely different Latin word, *sal*, salt), which I consider suitably bracing and briny for a county that styles itself 'by the Sea' in its very own anthem. So, for the purposes of this book, let us take salacious to mean lecherous in particular and reprehensible in general, with a light salty seasoning.

Deciding which individuals and events would be included was also an enterprise fraught with difficulties. There is an embarrassing number of scandals and naughtinesses to choose from and badly behaved characters can be found in the most unlikely corners of the county. Of course, there had to be a Sussex angle, but apart from that, it was quite a challenge. Anything so lost in time that no one can remember it was scratched, as was anything so new and sordid that it would only end in litigation, or anything illegal yet so boring that readers would slump over their afternoon oolong. Weird curses (with one exception) or ghosts (almost always a ploy by smugglers to keep their drop zones clear at night) were also right out. On the other hand, anything that was so juicy that it burst out of our county line and sprawled out onto the world stage was a given (step forward Lord Lucan, Eric Gill, the Piltdown Conspirators, Horatio Bottomley, Kitty O'Shea and Charles Parnell,

John George Haigh, and the Great Beast of Hastings). Also, as it is an offence to write a book about Sussex and knowingly exclude the Bloomsbury Group, they are in, although not in the form you may expect. And of course smugglers are compulsory. This is a slim volume and I have done my best but you can't please everyone, so apologies in advance if I have left out your favourite shocker.

Those that made the final cut have been divided up into five sections to make it easier to find what you want. Hanky Panky covers a spectrum of lewdness from incest to prurience, and the social spectrum from royalty to national artistic treasure. The Smuggling Game will prove to you once and for all that quaint Sussex villages have plenty to be ashamed about. Chicanery will leave you faintly embarrassed but perversely proud that Sussex is the home of such diverse and ingenious fraudsters as the Napoleon of Finance and the audacious Piltdown hoaxer. Murder anywhere is always shamingly enjoyable, but this Murder section shows you how Sussex does it with style; and finally the Cads & Bounders section rounds up a range of disparate reprobates for you to despair over.

While researching and writing this book I found out many things I am ashamed I did not already know. For example, I discovered that John George Haigh, the notorious acid bath murderer, sludged his last victim in Crawley, of all places (oh, the banality of evil), and was apprehended there; and that there were three Brighton trunk murders. And who would have thought that Eastbourne would be quite so blood-spattered; or that being brought up as a member of the Plymouth Brethren (George Haigh, Aleister Crowley, John Bodkin Adams) could turn you out quite so wrong. I hope that reading this will be as eye-popping for you as it has been for me writing it.

PART ONE

HANKY PANKY

As everyone knows, Brighton is the capital of hanky panky; it is, as Keith Waterhouse describes it, a town with 'the perennial air of being in a position to help the police with their inquiries' and it is where gentlemen used to go to manufacture sordid evidence so that their wives could divorce them. This is why it comes first in this list, but I don't want you to think that it holds the monopoly on smut; the whole county quivers with jiggery pokery and goings-on; there is even a special Sussex word for it: mollocking. This was coined by Stella Gibbons, and is the chief occupation of Seth Starkadder in *Cold Comfort Farm*, but Gibbons was really only creating a label for an ancient established Sussex tradition.

In this section I have aimed to keep things classy; there is no point in dwelling on rustic or proletarian filth when you have such splendid examples from royalty, the moneyed middle class and the artistic community to work with. (Wait till you read what Eric Gill got up to.) My one disappointment in this section is that the nation's great chronicler of hanky panky, D.H. Lawrence, lived in a cottage at Greatham, near Pulborough, for six months in 1915, but failed dismally to get up to anything notable, being respectably married to Frieda at the time, and too busy writing a short story ('England, My England') that denigrated his hosts, the Meynell family.

SUSSEX ROYALE

PRINNY IN BRIGHTON

Georgie Porgie, Puddin' and Pie, Kissed the girls and made them cry,
When the boys came out to play, Georgie Porgie ran away.

TRADITIONAL NURSERY RHYME

Unfortunately, and before pedants write in, these saucy couplets do not refer to our very own royal playboy, George IV, the king formerly known as Prinny, but they should. (If you are interested, the rhyme apparently refers to George Villiers, 1st Duke of Buckingham, a personage of enigmatic sexuality, and one of James I's numerous favourites; a very distant descendant, Frances Villiers, Countess of Jersey, was to become one of Prinny's mistresses, but that doesn't really count as a Sussex connection.) The words should fit because it was Prinny, eater of many pies, who single-handedly transformed Brighthelmstone, an unassuming small town on the south coast devoted to healthful sea-bathing, fishing and smuggling, into Brighton, the hanky-panky capital of the British Isles.

The prince & the widow

It was not entirely his fault. It shows how even the best regulated families can produce black sheep and how the devil makes work for idle hands. Born in 1762, the first son of George III, George Augustus Frederick, Prince of Wales, was an impulsive, self-indulgent hedonistic dandy with attention deficit disorder and a genius for spending money. When he was 21, he was given a grant of £60,000 from Parliament and a £50,000 annual allowance from his father; he moved into Carlton House, London, and began living a life of profligate luxury that would make the average premiership footballer look parsimonious. Pretty soon he was £160,000 in debt. Good going, what? He began hanging round with radical Whig politicians such as Charles James Fox, much to his father's disapproval; and worse than anything, after dalliances with a string of mistresses, including the Countess of Jersey (see above), he fell in love with glamorous, twice-widowed Maria

Fitzherbert, and they apparently married secretly in December 1785. The scandalous thing was not that she was a widow, nor that she was six years older than him, but that he had married her without his father's consent and, worse than anthing, that she was a Roman Catholic. Under the Act of Settlement of 1701, a royal who married a Catholic would be unable to succeed to the throne. So the marriage was kept 'secret', at least from the public. Mrs Fitzherbert promised never to mention it (and she didn't) and resigned herself to a twilight life, neither wife nor mistress. Over the years, Prinny repeatedly abandoned her but always returned, and probably did really love her but just lacked the necessary commitment muscle.

It was just after he had met Mrs Fitzherbert that Prinny discovered Brighton in 1783. It had already been popular in a very low key way as a health resort for the worried wealthy when he hit town, probably to get away from the beady disapproval of his father and indulge his taste for wine, women, song, French cuisine, smart clothes, gambling and patronising the arts. As an anonymous wit in *The Times* once wrote, he would always prefer 'a girl and a bottle to politics and a sermon'.

A year later he sent his cook, Louis Weltje, down to Brighton to find a house for him. As soon as he got there, he ordered it to be made over into a neoclassical marine Pavilion. Of course with Prinny came a syco-phantic entourage of dashing blades in knowing gigs, all of whom adored dicin' and drinkin' and eatin' and dressin' up as much as he did. He formed a kind of alternative court, with himself as the First Gentleman of Europe; it must have been like a bunch of trustafarians hitting a hapless Thai beach settlement in their gap year.

London-by-the-Sea

Prinny and his posse took over the Steyne (now Steine) as a kind of personal sports arena. I suppose you could say that it was his theme park. When Prinny had the Pavilion first remodelled by Henry Holland in 1787, he ordered his bedroom to be designed and hung with mirrors so that he could lay at his ease yet still watch whatever disport there was on the Steyne. There were races of all kinds. Officers and gentlemen, mounted on other officers and gentlemen, raced against 80-year-olds. Young women were tempted into bouncing along in races for the prize of a new hat. Races were run backwards. Sometimes a stag would be released and hunted down. The prince took potshots at doves.

With the arrival of Prinny, Brighton was instantly established as the place to be. After all, doctors recommended it. The aristocracy flocked. Elegant villas were built to accommodate them, hotels for the less committed. There were theatres, concerts, and masquerades. Between what is now New Road, the Pavilion, Church Street and North Street stretched an area known as the Promenade Grove, where nightly masquerades were held, bands played, fireworks whizzed and disguised revellers flitted naughtily between the trees. It was indeed London by the Sea, without the rules. Brighton became a byword for fast living. In *Pride and Prejudice* (written 1796-97) Jane Austen tells us all we need to know about what will happen to foolish, headstrong Lydia Bennett when she despatches her to Brighton.

A second wedding

One of the reasons that Prinny liked Brighton so much was because he could be with Mrs Fitzherbert in public, and in the Pavilion. In Brighton the secret marriage wasn't all that secret, Mrs F. was known as Mrs Prince to her intimates. Urban legend has it that there was a secret passage linking the Pavilion to her own house (now the YMCA!) when it was built in 1804.

However, all the wild living, arts patronage, theatre-going, drinking, gambling and frittering away jewels on pretty women added up, and by 1795 Prinny was in trouble again. Parliament would no longer wear his drunken-sailor style spending and his father would only bail him out on condition that he married to secure a legitimate heir. Prinny submitted gracelessly and in 1795 married his cousin Caroline of Brunswick. He loathed her at first sight, and she him apparently, although they managed to produce a child, Charlotte. A year later they separated inimically. Prinny slipped back down to the lotus-eating life in Brighton and, after a few diversions, into the arms of Mrs Fitzherbert.

Regency & the crown

It was not to last. The King had been suffering from bouts of what is now believed to be porphyria, and he and Parliament decided that there should be a mechanism in place to preserve government protocol if he were incapacitated; so in 1811 Prinny was elevated to Prince Regent. It gave him more power to interfere, and more money, but did not make him any more frugal or responsible. Mrs Fitzherbert broke with him, possibly because he was now likely to be king, or maybe because of more mistresses, but he continued to grant her an annual allowance. He comforted himself with his sartorial guru Beau Brummell, the man who introduced the idea of daily shaving, bathing and cleaning of teeth, who advised him to desist from wearing wigs and rouge, to wear dark clothes, knee breeches, and a cravat to cover up his double chins. He also began to fiddle, or rather got his architect to fiddle, with the Pavilion; in 1815, John Nash remodelled it into the biscuit-tin extravaganza of fanciful Indo-Chinoiserie we know today, and architectural tinkering and finessing went on until 1823.

By this time, George III had died and Prinny became king (in 1821) as George IV. He continued to visit the Pavilion until 1827. He was now a very fat boy, and addicted to laudanum. His coronation, although costly, was popular with the masses, but he soon lost public support, and spent most of his life in bed at Windsor, getting rounder and rounder. When he died in 1830 it was discovered that he had kept all of Mrs Fitzherbert's letters and still wore a locket of her hair.

There is no doubt that he behaved badly. But without him Brighton would not be what it is today, a place so geared to tolerant hedonism and the pursuit of style that it is almost impossible to behave in any way that would shock the inhabitants into raising so much as an eyebrow.

Just think what might have been if he had chosen Worthing instead.

More Salacious Detail

❯ *Prinny invented a new kind of shoe buckle to help keep buckle-makers in work*

❯ *Mrs Fitzherbert, who died in 1837, is buried at the church of St John the Baptist, Kemp Town*

THE DITCHLING DEGENERATE

ERIC GILL 1882-1940

*'What marvellous thing was this that suddenly transformed a
mere water tap into a pillar of fire...and water into an elixir of life.'*

ERIC GILL

That is the teenage Arthur Eric Rowton Gill registering in his diary his delight at the multi-tasking glory of his own penis, and it kind of sets the tone for his whole erotomane life.

Born the second child and eldest son of a clergyman in Brighton in 1882, Eric and the rest of the large (11 children) and genteelly impoverished family moved to Chichester 15 years later, where he studied at the Technical and Art School. In 1900 he went to London as an apprentice to a firm of ecclesiastical architects, but got bored and took up evening classes in calligraphy and stone carving. He became an undisputed master of linear expression. You are looking at his work right now, as this book is set in two of his iconic typefaces, Perpetua (1925) and Gill Sans (1927-30).

Art & filth

Gill was unquestionably a fine artist, sculptor, carver in stone and wood, letter-cutter, calligrapher and typographer, but let other pens dwell on his prolific artistic achievements. We are here for the filth and since 1989, when his biographer Fiona MacCarthy revealed what he had so meticulously noted down in his diaries, it's a lot saltier than suspected, indeed so reprehensible that in 1998 there was a petition to take down his *Stations of the Cross* series of reliefs in Westminster Cathedral. We can be proud, in a perverse way, that most of it took place in Sussex.

In 1904, Gill married Ethel Hester Moore (known as Mary), the daughter of the sacristan of Chichester Cathedral, and they lived in Battersea and Hammersmith for a bit, hanging round with the Arts and Crafts groups who flourished there. This was where he had a fling with the housemaid Lizzie, noting in his diary on June 14th 1906 that it was his 'first time of fornication since marriage'. It wasn't his last.

Presumably, this was also where he picked up his ideas about the artistic commune which, like all communes, usually means a group of subservient females and deferential males, or disciples, and one alpha male; more like a pride, really. In 1907, the Gills were back in Sussex, setting up just such a commune – 'a cell of good living in the chaos of the world' – in a house called Sopers in Ditchling, where Eric could expound his theories on art and the divine, and fulminate against contraception, the horror of 20th-century mechanistic culture, and the wearing of tight trousers that constricted and degraded 'man's most precious ornament'. When he later joined a lay order of Dominican monks, he used to go commando, and often wore a loose monkish robe that blew about in the wind to reveal his manhood to the passing crowd.

Sex in stone

It was at Ditchling that Gill took up sculpture and created, among other things, *Votes for Women*, a carving of explicit intercourse with the woman on top (remember, the suffragist movement was at its height). It was bought by local Bloomsbury Groupie John Maynard Keynes for £5; when he was asked how his staff would react to it, he replied that they had been trained not to believe their eyes. A far bigger enterprise was a beautiful life-size relief of Gill's sister Gladys and her husband Ernest Laughton in a state of connubial exuberance, carved between 1910-11. Gill called this, with admirable directness, *Fucking*, and for a while it belonged to the Lewes art collector Edward Perry Warren, he who had commissioned *The Kiss* from Rodin (*see p. 28*). Somehow, by the time it was found languishing in a boathouse in Birchington-on-Sea, Kent (how?), and bought by Tate Britain it had been uptitled to *Ecstasy* and was the subject of much learned discussion about how strongly Gill had been influenced by Indian temple sculptures. It wasn't filth, you understand, it was spiritual; and so it is, but it's hard to keep that in mind when you know that Gill was still sleeping with his sister when he created the piece, had been doing so since they were siblings together squashed up in the little terraced family home on Chichester's North Walls, and would continue to do so for most of their lives.

Catholic tastes

In 1913, finding the C. of E. too anodyne, Gill converted to Catholicism. Being Gill, he spent the instruction period all converts must undergo carving a life-size replica in marble of his own genitals. With no sense of irony, he also took to wearing the girdle of the Dominican order over his roomy robe, referring to it as his 'chastity belt'. With even less sense of irony he moved his family and entourage into Hopkin's Crank, a ram-shackle cottage with some attendant sheds on Ditchling Common because he believed, apparently not perceiving any contradiction in terms, that there could 'be no mysticism without asceticism'. His three daughters and adopted son were home-schooled, and did not mingle with the world. It is now apparent why they didn't. Perversely, while being set apart from the world, they also became a kind of tourist attrac-tion, especially for Catholics, who would call in to watch them at their artistic endeavours, living on wholesome home-baked bread.

After World War I, Gill set up the Guild of St Joseph and St Dominic, a mixture of arts and crafts, unorthodox religion and alternative lifestyles that would today be seen as a cult. During their 11 years on the Common, Gill made a series of undeniably exquisite life drawings of his teenage daughter Petra; it's only now that we know that he was sleeping with his two elder daughters at the time that the images carry a heavier load.

When in 1924 even the slow-moving folk of Ditchling got fed up with the goings on up at Hopkin's Crank, Gill shifted family, work-shops, Guild and dogs to mid Wales, settling in a ruined Benedictine monastery (what else?) at Capel-y-ffin in the Black Mountains near Abergavenny. Despite his expressed preference for apartness from the world, it turned out to be a little too remote from his client base – the Gill brand was very successful – so after four years the whole caboodle relocated to a house called Pigotts, in High Wycombe, Buckinghamshire.

A tarnished treasure

Gill became one of Britain's most respected and popular artists: his was the lettering on the war memorials in most towns and villages;

in 1932 he created a group of sculptures, *Prospero and Ariel*, for the headquarters of the fledgling BBC. (He worked on them *in situ* in his signature flowing robes, and shocked many an unwary passer-by when the wind rattled the scaffolding poles); in 1937 he designed a postage stamp; in 1938, he produced *The Creation of Adam*, three bas-reliefs in stone for the League of Nations building in Geneva. His autobiography, published just after his death in 1940, was reprinted 13 times. He was a National Treasure.

Then in the early 1980s his diaries, currently in the University of California in Los Angeles, were made public. In them he had noted down, in precise detail and exquisite calligraphy, all his sexual adventures – wives, sisters, daughters, men, women, friends, husbands of friends and dogs – that the full extent of his peculiarities was revealed. Yes, dogs. His diary entry for December 8th 1929 reads: 'Bath. Continued experiment with dog after and discovered that a dog will join with a man.' That this shocker did not actually dent his artistic reputation says a lot for his genius. And, to be fair, Gill appeared to sincerely believe that 'sexual intercourse is the very symbol for Christ's love for His Church, His Bride' and the metaphor of Christ as bridegroom is well established in the Catholic tradition. But you can't help thinking that he would have been better advised leaving the idea in the metaphorical realm. Especially when it came to the dog.

More Salacious Detail

◉ *Ditchling Museum, Church Lane, Ditchling, East Sussex BN6 8TB, houses the collection of the Guild of St Joseph and St Dominic. Website: www.ditchling-museum.com*

◉ *Eric Gill, Fiona MacCarthy, Faber & Faber, 2003*

◉ *The Eric Gill Society, a resource for the work and history of Eric Gill. Website: www.ericgill.org.uk*

IN STEYNING, IN SECRET

CHARLES PARNELL & MRS O'SHEA

*'When I married him he struck me as one of the
happiest bridegrooms I had ever married.'*

EDWARD CRIPPS, SUPERINTENDENT REGISTRAR, STEYNING

It is always the quiet ones. Who would have thought that one of the greatest political scandals to rock late 19th-century Britain would have had as its epicentre the little town of Steyning, West Sussex, whose only previous claim to fame was that it allegedly had been the last place in England to publicly burn a witch? It goes to show you never can tell.

The event that shoved Steyning on to the world stage was the secret marriage of Charles Parnell, the charismatic leader of the Irish Nationalist Movement, and his mistress Katherine (Kitty) O'Shea on June 25th 1891.

The 'uncrowned king'

Described by William Gladstone as the most remarkable man he had ever met, Charles Stewart Parnell almost achieved independence for Ireland, and certainly designed the template for a modern parliamentary political party, for which he received iconic status in his home country. Parnell was born in 1846 in County Wicklow, the son of Anglo-Irish Protestant landowners (the very class of people he sought to destroy). In 1875, he was elected as MP for County Meath representing the Home Rule Party, and began his meteoric rise and rise. He was a smart and wily tactician, and soon allied with the more radical supporters of Home Rule in the house. Together they started a campaign of obstructivism (destabilising parliamentary progress via technical procedures) to make the Irish presence felt. In 1877 he became president of the Home Rule Confederation, and later leader of the Irish National Land League, and began to pull together a difficult alliance of moderates, hardliners, tenant farmers and the middle classes; he travelled to the USA to seek funds and support, which he got, and so impressed everybody that he began to be referred to as 'the uncrowned king of Ireland'.

In 1880, there was a general election, and the Liberals, led by Gladstone, won. Parnell was returned as MP for Cork. Gladstone enacted the Land Act, but brutal evictions continued, so Parnell and his group encouraged civil disobedience (boycotts and rent strikes). They were arrested in 1881 and jailed for 'sabotaging the Land Act'. Ever the politician, Parnell made a deal with the government while in Kilmainham Gaol. The deal was brokered by one of Parnell's aides, Captain William O'Shea (remember the name) and resulted in the Kilmainham Treaty that offered an end to civil disobedience in return for the settlement of the rent arrears problem. Parnell was out in six months. He cut the ties with the more militant arm of his supporters and resumed his seat in Parliament, where he set about building the Irish Parliamentary Party (a rebranded Home Rule Party), generally seen as the first modern political party, with a party line, a whip, and an efficient structure.

Parnell was back on course for success. That the Irish Home Rule Bill of 1886 was scuppered by a mixture of outraged Irish Unionists in alliance with Tory anti-Home Rulers and disaffected Liberals is another story.

Two funerals & a wedding

Enough of politics, we are here for the scandal, and that is, after all, what did for this great man in the end. It was all down to sex, sleaze and vengeful journalists.

In May 1882, Thomas Henry Burke, the Permanent Under Secretary in the Irish Office, and the Chief Secretary for Ireland, Lord Frederick Cavendish, were stabbed and slashed to death in Phoenix Park, Dublin. The murders were claimed by the Irish National Invincibles, a group of Fenian activists. The perpetrators were caught and hanged at Kilmainham, and Charles Parnell had publicly condemned the murders. However, in 1887, *The Times* claimed to have found letters that proved he secretly supported the murders. These were forgeries created by an embittered ex-Parnellite journalist, Richard Piggott. There was an official enquiry, and much to his political enemies' dismay, Parnell was exonerated. He received a standing ovation in the House of Commons and promptly sued *The Times* for libel and won £5,000 out of court.

So you can see *The Times* would be irked, looking for revenge. And it got its chance a year later. Captain William O'Shea, last seen setting up the Kilmainham Treaty, served divorce papers on his estranged wife, Katherine O'Shea, citing Charles Stewart Parnell as co-respondent.

The end of the affair

Katherine O'Shea first met Charles Parnell in 1880, when she was married to Captain O'Shea although they were separated. As the niece of Lord Hatherly, Gladstone's Lord Chancellor, she was well placed to act as a liaison between Parnell and Gladstone during the run-up to the Irish Home Rule Bill of 1886. Although that failed, obviously the liaison prospered. Parnell was unmarried and fell deeply in love; they began a long affair, meeting in various houses in Brighton, which Katherine knew well as she had lived in Patcham with Captain O'Shea and her first son had been born there. The affair flourished, Katherine bore Parnell three children (born in 1882, 1883 and 1884) and in the summer of 1886 he moved into her house in Eltham. Captain O'Shea knew about the affair and challenged Parnell to a duel, but this was probably all bluster, and Katherine later claimed that he had encouraged the affair, thinking that it would be politically helpful to him.

But in 1890, when Parnell was at his zenith, O'Shea chose to file for divorce. This could have been a belated political revenge – O'Shea must have known that it would split the alliance of Catholics and Protestants that Parnell had so assiduously welded together in the IPP – but I fear it was all about the money, as it so often is. Katherine and her children had been living on money supplied by her rich aunt, and had expectations of a healthy legacy. However, when the aunt died in 1889, the will was contested, the money went to other relatives and Katherine got none of it. Captain O'Shea had perhaps been looking for a good fat pay-off for his silence. Realising he had nothing to lose, and despite his religious alignment, he went public on the affair and began divorce proceedings in November 1890.

News of the affair was not a surprise to many politicians, but both the English and the Irish nations were rocked. The press, led by *The Times*, went to town, jeering at Parnell for standing by his lover and insulting Katherine by calling her Kitty (at the time a synonym for prostitute). The Irish Parliamentary Party fell apart as Parnell's one-time friends deserted him and he was forced to resign as leader of the party he had created. Nevertheless, when the divorce was finalised, he applied, in person, for a special marriage licence in Steyning. No church would marry the couple.

Why Steyning?

Because they wanted to avoid publicity and the 1890s' version of the paparazzi; they had been living next door to each other in Walsingham Terrace, Aldrington, which made them eligible for a Steyning wedding. If they had gone to Brighton, no doubt the press pack would have been on them like wolves on the fold. It was a good choice, because neither the registrar Mr Spearing nor the Superintendent Registrar, the estimable Mr Edward Cripps, when offered the customary slush money, would spill any beans beyond the bare authorised press statement. Steyning can be very proud. *The Times* was extremely snotty about it, claiming that its quiet secrecy implied even more buried scandal.

As for the wedding it was a very quiet affair. Parnell and Katherine set off from Walsingham Terrace at 6.30 on the morning of June 25th 1891 in a pony cart, with Katherine at the reins. Their witnesses went by train (yes, Steyning had a station then; the railway had come to the town in 1861 and stayed until it fell to the Beeching axe in 1966). The ceremony took place at 9 o'clock, and then the couple returned to Aldrington. Charles tried to resuscitate his career, but ill health took hold of him, and on October 16th, his life's work ruined but his love intact, he died aged only 45, with Katherine beside him.

More Salacious Detail

❯ Captain O' Shea died in 1905; he had been living at 19 Lansdowne Place, Hove

❯ Katherine Parnell left Brighton in 1892; she died 1921 at Littlehampton and is buried in the municipal churchyard there

❯ Katherine and Charles stayed occasionally at 39 Bedford Square and Medina Terrace, Hove

❯ You can see a copy of the marriage certificate at Steyning Museum.
   Website: www.steyningmuseum.org.uk

A SUSSEX SOAP OPERA

THE CONFUSED BLOOMSBERRIES

'The older one grows, the more one likes indecency.'

VIRGINIA WOOLF

I know, I know, not the Bloomsberries again. (It's what they called themselves, don't blame me). What would have happened if Vanessa Bell and Virginia Woolf had chosen a different county for their rustic bolt holes? East Sussex would have lost a lucrative tourist revenue stream, but Berwick church may have been spared its grey-and-dead salmon pink *trompe-l'oeuil* makeover. You can probably tell I can't be doing with them, but they loom large in the county's cultural landscape, and it is compulsory for every book on Sussex to include them.

They are in the hanky-panky section because their lives, when unwound from literary and artistic theory and practice, and the philosophical thought of G.E. Moore, are just like a soap opera (albeit one for the smart upper middle classes), and the essence of all good soap operas is hanky panky and goings-on in the woodshed with people you shouldn't be with. Quentin Bell (son of Vanessa) himself doubted if 'any group has ever been so radical in its rejection of sexual taboos'.

The second tenet of soap aesthetic is that everybody should either be related in some way or have gone to school with each other, that strangers are not welcome (especially if they are Dora Carrington) and that the outside world should rarely impinge. The 'Berries transferred their leftfield Boho bubble intact from London to Cold Comfort Farm, Sussex. Apart from Vanessa's servant Nelly (such a treasure!), the native inhabitants of Firle and Charleston were non-speaking background artistes, as interesting as the sheep on the beacon. The third tenet of soap is that there must be a matriarch and that she should try to control everyone's lives, in this case by painting their furniture when they least expected it.

What would the Bloomsberry story board look like? The beautiful Stephens sisters (Virginia the career bluestocking and Vanessa the artistic matriarch) storm the salons of London; that's two fecund story arcs set up immediately. The artist marries suave, dashing but no-good Clive Bell, an art critic, presumably so he can spend time barking about the significance of form at her. Of course the marriage does not last. After two children Clive slopes off to be caddish in Europe and drop back into the story whenever the plot line needs juicing up. Vanessa settles down in the country with Bell's homosexual friend Duncan Grant, who fathers her daughter Angelica. She is born on Christmas Day, and David Garnett, her father's bisexual lover, 22 at the time, swears to marry her when she is old enough. And he does, but not before Vanessa has decided the wedding eve is just the right time to tell her that her father is not really Clive but gay Uncle Duncan, the ex-lover of the man she is about to marry. Cue dramatic drums.

Meanwhile, over at Rodmell, Virginia and Leonard Woolf have set up a slightly smaller arrangement (all soaps need rival loci). Their USP is that they are both writers, introducing a useful strand of domestic tension. After some unspecified unpleasant childhood experience (to be developed later) Virginia is wary of sex, and so it is a *mariage blanc* for poor Leonard, but in case we get bored with restraint, Virginia has a passionate fling with eccentric posh gardener, Vita Sackville-West.

Members of the two households are forever furthering the plot by bicycling over to misunderstand each other or writing ambiguous notes. There are frequent family parties to bring everyone together for a good row, and every now and then, when the storyline needs ventilating, favourite characters drop in (Roger Fry, Vanessa's lover and work colleague, for some erotic undertones, languid satirist Lytton Strachey for comic effect) and the occasional megastar turns up. (*Hola* Señor Picasso, passionate artistic genius, have you met legendary bisexual economist, John Maynard Keynes?)

You see, it's easy. Try it yourself.

More Salacious Detail

❯ *Go and see the Bloomsberry set for yourself at Monk's House and Charleston.*
Websites: www.nationaltrust.org.uk/main/w-vh/w-visits/w-findaplace/w-monkshouse/
and www.charleston.org.uk

NAUGHTINESS IN NUTLEY

MR MORRISS WALKS THE DOG

*'Young girls of gentle birth required to look after large dogs in the country;
live in; experience unnecessary, commonsense essential.'*

THE TIMES, 1925

In the early 1920s, Mr Hayley Morriss, a 37-year-old businessman of independent if dubious means returned from Shanghai to England with his fortune (and, as you will see, a voracious appetite) to take up the life of an English squire. He swiftly snapped up the estate of Pippingford Park, Nutley, at a bankruptcy sale. He settled in with his wife Madeleine and entered into the spirit of things. March 1924 saw him patenting an automatic pig feeder in his guise as gentleman farmer; in the same year he was mingling with the mighty in the newly instituted Irish Wolfhound Association, whose extremely toff vice-presidents were the Duchess of Hamilton and Brandon, the Duchess of Wellington, the Marquess of Londonderry, the Countess of Limerick and Lord Waring. Morriss presented two cups, the Mohawk Cup for the whitest dog and the Height Cup for the tallest beast.

He must have let his passion for large dogs get out of hand as he was soon forced to advertise for assistance (*see above*). He needed help with all the wolfhounds and only posh young gels would do. The young ladies flocked, but when they were taken on they discovered that there was a whole other meaning to the term walking the dog. You see, it was not just big dogs that tickled Mr M.'s fancy, but also young ladies, most of them under age. Apparently, he used to go round to say goodnight to them all personally; it must have been like some red light version of the Waltons. And before you ask, Mrs Morriss not only knew about it, she helped him procure the girls, so don't go feeling sorry for her.

Of course you cannot be running a house of ill repute in Nutley without the villagers getting to know about it; the gossip flowed and the dogwalkers blabbed. Did Mr Morriss think no one would notice? Or not understand that what was, maybe, par for the course in Shanghai would not wash in Sussex? In best tabloid tradition, the police swooped and just before Christmas in 1925, the Morrisses found themselves in the dock at Lewes Assizes charged with 22 counts of offences against young girls. They pleaded not guilty but during the course of the four-day trial it became apparent that not only were they very guilty indeed but that an in-house supply of kennel maids had not sated what the judge called Mr Morriss's 'loathsome lust'. He and Madeleine had also gone out cruising the streets of Brighton in their Rolls-Royce looking for fresh meat, and picked up two young ladies for dinner and a proposition.

It also became clear that Hayley Morriss hadn't been a very effective evil mastermind. Some of the young canine lovers were very upset but a few tougher cookies gave as good as they got, including one who wanted £1,000 and a ticket to California to shut her up; the girls had also been using the phone, and Morriss had been obliged to instruct the Nutley postmistress Ethel Whitewood only to accept calls from the house made by a man.

Even so, Mr Justice Avory took an extremely dim view of it all and once the jury had found the pair guilty in just 17 minutes, sent Mr Morriss down for three years, two of them with hard labour, and ordered him to pay £1,000 in costs. Mrs Morriss did some impressive swooning in the dock (she had once been a not-very-successful actress) and got off with only nine months as it was felt that she had been coerced by her husband.

The county was deliciously scandalised by the bizarre activities at Nutley. Best of all the Bloomsberries took it up. Mr and Mrs John Maynard Keynes, no less, wrote a spoof version of the scandal to be acted at one of the set's regular home theatrical evenings. In this version, Clarissa Dell (Vanessa Bell) is seduced by Mr Maley Horace (guess who) with an invitation to gaze at his Cezanne, take a peep at his Giotto, and redesign 'Pippington' House.

I expect it went down a storm on the night.

More Salacious Detail

◉ *Pippingford Park was once owned by a soldier and maintains its military connection as a training ground for the MOD and a favourite venue for re-enactment societies and film-makers. Website: www.pippingford.co.uk*

NO KISS FOR LEWES

NED WARREN v MISS K. FOWLER-TUTT

'I am much inclined to it.'

EDWARD PERRY WARREN

This is a tale of what happens when aesthetics crash into respectability, with a capital R: not so much hanky panky as anti-panky. Edward Perry ('Ned') Warren was an exotic flower in Lewes at the turn of the 20th century. A rich, eccentric American aesthete (Harvard and Oxford), Warren had been obsessed with the Classical Ideal – especially the Greek notion of masculine love – since the days of his youth when he had mooned about his Massachusetts mansion in a home-made toga. Warren was able to live the dream thanks to family wealth (based on paper milling) and toured Europe with his lover John Marshall collecting exquisite antiquities, many of which now form the basis of collections in the Boston Museum of Fine Arts and the Metropolitan Museum of Art in New York.

In 1890, Warren leased, then bought, Lewes House (to whose many rooms, stables and paddock he was 'much inclined') and created 'a monkish establishment where women were not welcomed'. Here he lived in splendour with John Marshall, a collection of young men, a stable full of Arab horses and six St Bernard dogs. This 'brotherhood of men' wandered about the town dressed in exotic garments, spoke Greek among themselves and photographed each other frolicking in the Lewes Corporation Swimming Pool. Artists and interesting persons, including, inevitably, the Bloomsberries, flocked to their many parties. One of the artists on Warren's guest list was the French sculptor Auguste Rodin.

Warren very much admired one of Rodin's works, *The Kiss*, but when he put in a bid, he found it was not for sale as it was part of a commission for the French government. Undeterred, he commissioned a copy, specifying one condition, namely that the genitals of the man should be 'complete' and sculpted in the Classical Greek tradition to be proud and prominent, not hidden behind bourgeois drapery.

But when the finished work was delivered (two years late) in 1904, Warren stuck it in the stable for a decade. This may have been because it was too big to fit in the house, but it was more likely to have been because the hotly anticipated genitals were not at all tumescently proud and Greek but rather disappointingly limp and sausagey. Then in 1907 Warren was left broken-hearted when John Marshall not only went straight but rubbed salt in the wound by marrying one of Warren's cousins; possibly the sight of heterosexual lovers embracing, even in chilly marble, became unbearable to poor Ned. In 1914 he presented the sculpture to the town of Lewes to be displayed in the town hall.

And was the town grateful for the gift of this masterpiece? Do I really need to tell you? Enter Miss Kate Fowler-Tutt, a local headmistress. She became the rallying point for the town's Puritan Tendency and Busybody Faction. They campaigned vigorously for the sculpture's removal, on the grounds that one look at a nude couple embracing would inflame the lustful passions of the soldiers billeted in Lewes wait- ing to be shipped across to the Flanders killing fields and drive them into depravity. I would have thought that something so life affirming would have been good for their spirits before they marched off to their doom, but Miss F.-T. knew better. Her energetic lobbying eventually won the day; first the sculpture was corralled by railings, and then shrouded in a sheet (what could be more titillating?) and finally, in 1917, it was thrust gracelessly back at its donor. Not Lewes's finest hour.

The Kiss spent another decade in the Lewes House stables, until Warren's death in 1928. His heir, Harry Thomas, tried to auction it at Gorringes, but it did not meet the reserve. After some time in obscu- rity, it was loaned to the Tate Gallery, who finally bought it in 1955. In 1999, it came back to Lewes and spent the summer in the Town Hall on exhibition, defiantly unshrouded. Nobody protested, and neither did anyone become inflamed by lust. Bit of a shame, really.

More Salacious Detail

❯ *Under the pen name of Arthur Lyon Raile, Warren wrote several books on the subject of gay love, including* Itamos *(1903) and* The Defence of Uranian Love *(1928-30).*
Miss Fowler-Tutt wrote a book called The Handkerchief Song: An Action Song *(1899)*

PART TWO

THE SMUGGLING GAME

I was going to call this section Stop Thief, but all the robberies in the county were kind of dull or mechanical and the robbers had no class, so I have stuck to what it seems Sussex did (and maybe still does) best: smuggling. There were times in the mid-18th century when the county was indistinguishable from 1920s Chicago or modern-day Compton. All those quaint beamed old pubs, tearooms, gift shops and themed experiences are built on blood. And tea, actually. Rum, brandy and silk are all very well but heavy; tea (which was taxed at an extortionate 119 per cent to pay for various wars) was light, lucrative, easy to transport and could be easily sold by respectable London merchants. Some smugglers even insured their cargoes at Lloyds. And you thought drug barons were a modern phenomenon.

As you couldn't move in the county for smuggling companies, many of whom worked in uneasy alliance with each other when it was in their interest, I have narrowed it down a bit: here are the cool brains of Alfriston, the heavies of Hawkhurst, the mad axemen of Hastings and the individual mastermind of Highdown Hill. And don't get sanctimonious, they only got away with it because everybody colluded and nobody liked paying taxes.

DOWNTOWN ALFRISTON

STANTON COLLINS & JEVINGTON JIG

'Watch the wall my darling, while the Gentlemen go by.'

RUDYARD KIPLING, *A SMUGGLER'S SONG*

It would be hard to imagine a more picturesque, genteelly English village than Alfriston; it is straight out of central casting, with its half-timbered pubs, quaintly slanting houses, cottage gardens and dear little shops where you can pick up essentials like organic chilli and beetroot chocolate or hand-crafted Sussex trugs. In fact, it is so all-round gorgeous that tourists wear grooves in it. There is a particular point on the one route in and out where the road pinches so narrow that only one vehicle can pass at a time. Many a fat touristical bus gets wedged there in high summer. And you can't help thinking that if today's Alfristonians had blood in their veins rather than chamomile tea, those sitting-duck outlanders would be robbed blind as they sat: but that would be so 200 years ago.

Because 200 years ago, it used to be all smugglers round here. And that is because 200 years ago the Crowlink gap at Cuckmere Haven provided a cart-width route from Cuckmere Haven direct to Alfriston so that smuggled goods, particularly the fine brandy known as 'genuine Crowlink', (the tea trade being all over by 1794) could be ferried up to the town, stashed away and later distributed, using nothing more than the wile and cunning of the Alfriston gang and the connivance of all the villagers. Two hundred years ago, Alfriston was the badlands.

The Alfriston Gang was not the biggest in the hood, but it made a profit, which was the main thing in the economic downturn after the Napoleonic Wars, and it didn't get caught. The Mr Big was Stanton Collins, who also doubled as the town butcher. He owned Market Cross House (now a pub called Ye Olde Smugglers, how trite can you get?), old when he inherited it but precision-built for the smuggling trade. It had 21 rooms, six staircases and 48 doors – just the thing for leading excise men a merry French-farcical dance – hidey holes in the cellars and roof and, allegedly, escape tunnels that led to other houses and even as far as Wilmington, although that seems a bit of a stretch. Collins and the gang pretty much ran Alfriston; when to Collins's disapproval a new minister took over at what is now the United Reform Church, the gang removed him, reinstalled the old one, and guarded the church to make sure he stayed there.

There was never enough evidence to pin on the Alfriston Gang, even though they certainly were involved in the death of a customs patrolman at Cuckmere Haven. To stop him interfering with a drop, they cunningly realigned the lumps of white chalk he used to mark the cliff's edge, and he walked straight off. What's worse, he managed to catch hold of the edge and hang on, only to get his fingers stamped on so that he fell to his death on the rocks. Yet Collins did eventually get his comeuppance when in 1831 he was arrested and tried for sheep stealing, or possibly barley rustling, and transported to Australia for seven years.

Jevington Jig

Stanton Collins may have been a smart villain but he wasn't very entertaining. Thirty or so years earlier, the area had had a much jollier villain in the leader of the Jevington Gang, who operated out of Birling Gap. He was Jevington Jig, aka James Petit, who also found time in his busy smuggling schedule to run the Eight Bells at Jevington (which of course also had smugglers' tunnels), and practise a smattering of horse thievin' and general larceny. He turned informer when times were hard, which was a bit foolhardy of him, and thought nothing of dressing up as a woman to get out of a tight spot (his boots gave him away). And, like Collins, he did not work alone; the tombs in Jevington churchyard were used to store contraband, Jevington rectory had suspiciously large cellars and there was a concealed cupboard and an underground passage in Filching Manor. They were all in on it.

More Salacious Detail

◈ The last member of the Alfriston Gang died in the workhouse at Eastbourne in 1890, aged 94

◈ It was not illegal to sell openly illegally imported brandy, and landlords used to advertise the fact that they had just got in a particularly good batch

RUXLEY'S CREW

THE HASTINGS CHOPBACKS

'Them that die'll be the lucky ones!'

ROBERT LOUIS STEVENSON, *TREASURE ISLAND*

Hastings fishermen are a small, tight-knit community, largely made up of a few inter-related families who have passed on the trade through many generations. Consequently, many of them share the same surname, and in many cases a family given name too. To avoid confusion, they are almost invariably known by their inventive nicknames, which range from the apt and amusing ('Old Mackerel' Gallop, 'Surly Dick' Phillips, 'Ickle' Curtis, 'Tightshin' Stonham and 'Tarbrush' Breeds, for example) to the downright baffling ('Diddyay' Veness, 'Oxo' Richardson, 'Didlo' Mann, 'Queerwhack' White and 'Whip-me-naked' Gallop – or maybe that one's not so baffling).

So if you mentioned Stephen Bourner on the Stade where the fishermen land their boats in the Old Town, you'd probably be met with a blank stare, but 'Ruxley' would probably get a smile of recognition. Because Ruxley (or Ruxey) Bourner was the leader of a notorious gang of Hastings 'free traders' in the 1760s, Ruxley's Crew, whose murderous exploits earned the local fisherfolk their bloodcurdling nickname.

Earning a living from fishing in small boats was even more difficult in the 18th century than it is today, and it is not surprising that many fishermen were tempted by more profitable pursuits such as smuggling and piracy. The Sussex coast was ideally situated to bring in goods unnoticed from the Continent, and the heavy maritime traffic up and down the Channel offered rich pickings to unscrupulous seafarers. In fact, during wars with the French (and we were often at war with the French) piracy was encouraged by government 'letters of marque', which licensed boats to attack enemy vessels and keep any booty they seized.

The Ruxley Crew didn't interpret this as law, however; more like guidelines. They didn't distinguish between times of war and peace, and certainly made no distinction between French and other foreign, or even British, craft. Their favourite trick was to set out in bad weather, ostensibly approaching a vessel in difficulty to offer assistance, then board it and lock the crew below decks. They then scuppered the boat and made off with the cargo, taking it back to Hastings where they could dispose of it through the smugglers' networks.

They met their match, though, and got their eventual comeuppance, when four of Ruxley's Crew attempted to board a Dutch boat off Beachy Head in August 1768. The Dutchmen fought back bravely, managing to repel the pirates, and even capture one of them, Stephen Taught. Ruxley returned with back-up, to find that the Dutch captain had ordered Taught's execution; his half-dead body was hanging from the rigging. The gang were not at all pleased by this barbarous treatment of their colleague, and sought their revenge. And, of course, the spoils.

Blinded with rage, the pirates fought with more than their usual ferocity, killing or maiming most of the crew, chopping the captain's back open with an axe and leaving him to die a slow and agonising death. (Hence the nickname.) Back home in Hastings they boastfully told the tale of their latest exploit, which, although it admirably enhanced their fearsome reputation, was to prove their last.

It was the last straw for law-abiding Hastonians. They had had enough of Ruxley and his thugs, and wanted a crackdown on their antics. The mayor proved ineffectual, and was attacked by outraged citizens who had themselves turned violent, so the government stepped in: a man-of-war patrolled the Hastings coast, and hundreds of dragoons were sent to round up the murderous brigands — and keep order amongst their many local sympathisers and the angry protesters. In a few months, 13 had been captured and were sent to the Old Bailey for trial, as it was thought a local jury would acquit them in fear of reprisals. At least four of Ruxley's Crew were hanged at Execution Dock in Wapping, the Admiralty's favoured location for the dispatch of pirates.

More Salacious Detail

◗ *The Ruxley Crew's savage attack on the Dutch captain so scandalised the good people of Sussex it earned them the nickname 'chopbacks' — a sobriquet that became applied by association to all the Hastings fishermen, and has stuck even to the present*

KINGS OF THE SOUTH SIDE

THE NOTORIOUS HAWKHURST GANG

'I like a nice cup of tea in the morning.'

A.P. HERBERT

Throughout the 18th century, most of Sussex was controlled by smuggling companies such as the Groombridge Gang, the Mayfield Gang, the Alfriston Gang and the Hooe Company – but the biggest, baddest bunch was the Hawkhurst Gang. Although technically based in Kent (though only just) they qualify for inclusion in a book about Sussex because of their activities in Rye and Robertsbridge. Between 1735 and 1749 they ran the south side. If you wonder where Al Capone got his ideas look no further. It was a big patch, stretching from Herne Bay in Kent to Poole in Dorset, but it was centred on the little village of Hawkhurst, about 10 miles (16 km) inland, because it happened to be on the road to London and all smuggled traffic from the Romney marshes funnelled through it. Location, location and location. In fact, the big money in smuggling was made by the gangs of inlanders who fronted up the cash and controlled distribution; all that wet romantic stuff with dark lanterns, moonless nights and little boats on the beach was usually outsourced to fishermen.

A villainous lair

The gang HQ was the Oak and Ivy Inn at Hawkhurst, but they also hung out at the Mermaid in Rye (it wasn't always all Mapp and Lucia campery) where they kept loaded pistols on the table while they drank, just to show the locals that they meant business. They were led by Thomas Kingsmill and the money man was Arthur Gray. So swaggeringly confident were they that they used their own houses – and even put up purpose-built 'smuggling facilities' for their work. They hid contraband in Highgate House, built tunnels, including one linking Hawkhurst Place with Island Pond, and established Tubs Lake and Smuggley (names a bit of a giveaway there, I feel) as staging posts for cargo en route from the coast. Business boomed so loudly, Arthur Gray was able to build a swish mansion at Seacox Heath. (Sea cocks was the nickname given to the smugglers.) It was called Gray's Folly – I am sure it would have had a swimming pool with a portrait of Arthur picked out in gold tiles if only such things had been available at the time – and included plenty of 'storage' and en suite hidey holes.

By 1740 the gang was so well established that they no longer needed to hide. They could get together a small army of 500 desperadoes in a couple of hours, and often did. A cargo of contraband tea they had hijacked and hidden in a barn in Etchingham was found and re-seized by excise officers. One of the gang found out that the consignment was on its way back to Hastings under armed guard. Appalled by such effrontery, he rounded up 30 of his colleagues to ambush the customs party at Silver Hill in Robertsbridge, where they already had a gang leader, John Amos, embedded. They chose a good spot – Silver Hill is very steep – and there was a furious drink-fuelled fight in which one exciseman, Thomas Carswell, was killed, and the dragoons guarding the merchandise were taken hostage.

The gang got away with it because most people were part of the smuggling game in some way, and nearly everybody drank tea; to make doubly sure, the Hawkhurst Gang was big on intimidation and threats, and burning down the houses of uppity magistrates. It must have been a bit like living in London when the Kray twins ruled; as long as you kept your nose clean, there would be no trouble, and they certainly kept the non-professional crime rates down.

The Battle of Goudhurst

However, the worm turned in 1747; the gang had spilled over into neighbouring Goudhurst where they swaggered about in the Star and Eagle Inn, and took whatever they wanted whenever they wanted it. The Goudhurstinistas got as mad as hell and did not want to take it any more, so went vigilante and challenged the Hawkhurt Gang, a very daring move. The Goudhurst Band of Militia was formed, led by an ex-soldier. By now far too big for his boots, and definitely not at home

to Mr Hubris, Thomas Kingsmill named the day for the showdown –
April 20th – handing the advantage to Goudhurst. When the Hawkhurst
Gang arrived, drunk and stripped to the waist, they were not prepared
for the organised resistance that met them, and were seen off. It was a
victory for village power.

This public routing of the seemingly invincible gang may have
been the tipping point, but the end came when they behaved so bar-
barically that even the most complacent and tea-addled villager could not
but protest. Previous gangs of smugglers had been violent if required,
but their usual MO was to tie up the enemy and remove their weapons.
What the Hawkhurst Gang did revolted people because it did not take
place during a raid, and although one of the victims was a customs
officer, the other was an innocent bystander trying to do the right thing.

Two murders too far

In September 1747 the Hawkhurst Gang was villainously duped out of
an anticipated cargo of two tons of tea when a customs cutter inter-
cepted a delivery from France and it was taken to Poole. Outraged, 60
members of the gang attacked the Customs House to reclaim their tea,
which they paraded back through Dorset and Hampshire to show how
hard and untouchable they were. The Customs Service were in their
turn outraged and offered a huge reward for their capture. There weren't
many takers, such was the fear that the gang engendered. Months went
past, and then it somehow came to official notice that poor doomed
Daniel Chater, a cobbler from Fordingbridge, had been seen talking to
gang member Jack Diamond, a friend of his. Jack had slipped a little
gift of a pack of tea to his old mate as the gang came through the town.
No doubt this counted as 'possession with intent to drink', as well as
consorting with known felons. Pressure was exerted. Chater must have
felt that he was between a rock and a hard place. Very reluctantly he
agreed to testify against the gang and was sent off to Chichester with
customs officer William Galley in a sort of early witness protection
scheme to lay a deposition before a Sussex magistrate. You can guess
what's coming next; hear those duelling banjos.

The pair stopped for the night at the White Hart at Rowland's Castle, near the Hampshire and Sussex border, and were obviously not too bright about keeping things dark. The landlady, mother of two strapping young smugglers, worked out who they were, raised the alarm and plied the pair with drink while she waited for the gang to arrive. Next morning, probably still severely hungover, Chater and Galley were dragged out of bed, horse whipped, tied naked to horses and forced to ride 15 miles (24 km) to the next village, Rake. Barely conscious from their beatings, they slid underneath the horses' bellies, so that their heads were pounded by the hooves. By the time they finally arrived, William Galley appeared to have died from this torture, so the Gang buried him. They chained poor Chater up in a barn, beat him some more, drank themselves legless at the Red Lion and then went home for a couple of days to establish alibis and decide what to do to make an example of the informer. When they returned, they carved Chater's face open, dangled him over a well by his neck then threw him in head first. When he still wouldn't die they hurled rocks at him until he did.

Retribution

When news of the two murders got out, at the same time as large rewards were mentioned, the locals decided that enough was enough, and people began to come forward to give evidence. They were encouraged by the actions of one of the gang who had been arrested, and offered bravely to name names in return for leniency. The bodies were found and it was discovered that poor Galley had been buried alive. Over the following six months, all the gang were taken. Eight of the ringleaders, including Gray and Kingsmill, were tried, sentenced to death by hanging, and their corpses dangled on gibbets in their own villages to discourage others.

The Hawkhurst Gang would ride no more.

More Salacious Detail

❿ Writer and politician Horace Walpole was visiting the area on the day of the ambush; he described Robertsbridge as a 'wretched village' and complained that all the beds at the inn 'were inhabited by smugglers, whom the people of the house call mountebanks'

THE JOLLY MILLER

JOHN OLLIVER OF HIGHDOWN HILL

' I am but mad north-northwest.'

WILLIAM SHAKESPEARE, *HAMLET, ACT IV, SCENE II*

Granted it appears that absolutely everybody in 18th-century Sussex from the top down was somehow involved in smuggling, and that even the excise men occasionally turned poachers, it was still technically illegal, and in some cases a hanging offence. How not to get caught? One enterprising Sussex smuggler (alleged!) chose the most effective methods known to magicians, conjurors, card sharps and other slippery customers: hide in plain view and misdirect the audience. And very successful he was too.

John Olliver (or Oliver) was the miller of Highdown Hill, near Ferring. Although it is statistically unlikely that he wasn't involved in smuggling, his cover was so good that to this day no one can be sure whether he was a major player in the 'free trade business' or just an amiable eccentric obsessed with the style of his own demise. We can't even check the windmill for clues as it is no longer there. But let's look at the evidence.

Born in 1709, John took over the business from his father Clement in 1750. The mill was set up high on the hill and commanded a clear view of the Channel; and anything in the Channel also commanded a clear view of it. Professional millers claim that this is a silly place to put a mill (far too exposed and draughty), but professional smugglers will point out that it is an ideal place to put a signalling tower. John was almost 40 when he took over from his father, and he did not move the mill, so it seems logical, Watson, that his father was also part of the local culture. John would have learned at his father's elbow how to fix the sails in a certain way to send warnings and pass on information to dark boats lurking in the offing. And this tells us it was a family business. If you look on the village rolls and censuses for the area, especially Angmering and Goring, you will find oodles of Ollivers, spelled in various ways; if you weren't born an Oliver or Olliver you almost always married one. What better security system do you need? Families do not give each other up to the authorities, at least not without other parts of the family finding out and doing something about it.

John set about cultivating his eccentric persona, being stout and jolly and given to japes and fixing charming but pointless weathervanes to his cottage. In 1763, he built himself a little shed a couple of hundred yards uphill from his actual home. He would go there every day to read his Bible. I point out to you that the Bible, being the book most people were likely to have, was an ideal source book for cipher codes. And those weathervanes on the roof of his cottage, no doubt with some mechanism that could work from inside, and visible from his shed? One showed a miller; when the wind blew his sack opened and he shovelled in flour; the other showed a smuggler being chased by an excise man, himself being chased by a crone with a broom. Tell me that is not a code.

If you were as good a lookout as J. Olliver obviously was you got a cut of the loot. Two years after building the shed, he got permission from his neighbouring landowner, William Richardson, to build himself a tomb, next to his shed. There was no reason not to build on his own land, and this was a great big stone and brick affair, but Mr Richardson gave permission without a murmur (dearie me, could he have known what was going on?). John built the tomb he would not need for another 30 years, but which would meanwhile make a great stash for contraband. He also made himself a coffin (how typically eccentric of him) but it had wheels on, was kept hidden under his bed, and had a spring device that could retract it instantly in case anyone came in and caught him considering his mortality.

He finally died rich in 1793, after a lifetime of not much milling; the coffin was painted white, it was carried by white-clad children, 2,000 of his intimate friends attended, and it descended into a drunken riot. Just the cover you need to clear away anything incriminating.

More Salacious Detail

❯ Legend has it that the ghost of John Olliver will appear if you run round the tomb seven times. Maybe the running opens a smugglers' tunnel

PART THREE

CHICANERY

This is a short section that, because of the profligate characters it features, seems larger than it actually is. (You see? Two lines in and we have arrived at tricksiness already.) It is a brief encounter 1) for legal reasons and 2) because I have avoided dreary and depressing fraudulence involving banks, hedge funds, or anonymous megacorps, terrible rippings off in which people lost everything, which isn't a bit funny. Chicanery is a French word meaning legal trickery, with a strong element of merry pranksterishness. A bit like shenanigans, but with more class. Our select fraudsters are world-class showmen all, who not only did it on a grand scale but were themselves larger than life and added greatly to the gaiety of the nation (not just the people of Sussex), and who understood the first rule of huckstering: people will happily conspire to be defrauded as long as they get some great entertainment in return.

FRAUDULENT FOSSILS

THE PILTDOWN HOAX

'The name of Charles Dawson is certain of remembrance. We do well to link his name to this picturesque corner of Sussex – the scene of his discovery.'

SIR ARTHUR KEITH

Palaeontology may seem to outsiders a harmless, and indeed rather boring, pursuit practised by earnest, academic gentlemen past their passionate prime. But that's a very mistaken impression – beneath the owlish veneer is a seething mass of nefarious goings-on prompted by jealousy, rivalry, revenge, jingoism, and a lust for fame and a place in the history books. Which is perhaps why it caught on so well in Sussex. In Sussex, at least, it is all the fault of Gideon Mantell (1790-1852), the Lewes gynaecologist and amateur fossil-hunter who is credited with discovering the first fossilised remains of a dinosaur in 1822. Deception is equally popular, it appears, as the fossil teeth were probably unearthed by his wife Mary, but Mantell took all the credit – although, to be fair, he did recognise their importance and correctly identify them as belonging to a Mesozoic reptile which he named Iguanodon. Mantell's medical career suffered as a result of his obsession with prehistory, and when he moved to Brighton in 1833, he managed to virtually bankrupt himself in what should have been a thriving practice. Brighton Council helped him set up his home as a museum, but he even turned this into a loss-making business, and only survived by selling, after a bit of haggling, his fossil collection to the British Museum. Mary left him (who can blame her?) and he moved to London – where he promptly got run over by a passing carriage on Clapham Common and became an opium addict as a result.

The wizard of Sussex

But Mantell's career was positively exemplary in comparison with the amateur palaeontologists who were to follow – especially Charles Dawson (1864-1916), hailed as the 'Wizard of Sussex' for his many important archaeological finds. Dawson was born in Hastings, and became a well-respected solicitor in Lewes, but was also an enthusiastic and (more worryingly) ambitious archaeologist. When he was only 21, he was elected 'a fellow of the Geological Society with a reputation for uncannily frequent and important discoveries around Sussex' – but it was never enough for him, and he longed for a spectacularly unique find that would earn him fame, fortune, a place in the history books, and maybe even a knighthood.

Name that skull

Spookily, his big break came not long after he had confided his ambitions to his friend Arthur Smith Woodward at the British Museum: the remains of an early hominid were found at Dawson's dig in a gravel pit at Piltdown in 1912. Amazing, what? The hunt for the 'missing link' proving Darwin's theories had been on since Neanderthal man was discovered in 1856, and several human ancestors were subsequently found in Europe and Asia. Dawson's find, fragments of a skull and a jawbone which he promptly dubbed *Eoanthropus dawsoni*, definitively showed the characteristics of both man and ape, and what's more, was British, by George, and showed that the sun wasn't yet setting on the Empire. And it wouldn't do Dawson's standing any harm either. Or at least, it wouldn't have done if it had been genuine.

Still, Dawson had his moment of glory, and died long before Piltdown Man was exposed as a fake (and a pretty crude one, at that). In fact, it fooled most of the experts for more than 40 years, and the perpetrators of the hoax have still not been conclusively identified. Could it have been Dawson, the respectable Sussex solicitor? Surely not... although inevitably suspicions were aroused, and further investigations into his remarkable catalogue of archaeological discoveries proved at least 38 of them to have been fakes. Dawson knew exactly what he was hoping to find – Piltdown Man fitted the bill perfectly, combining a human skull with an ape's mandible – and he also had the expertise to make a convincing forgery: in this case marinating the bones to simulate fossilisation and the staining of age, and filing the teeth to disguise the modernity of the orang-utan jaw.

Hunt the hoaxer

Dawson isn't the only person in the frame, however, as a number of other palaeontologists with axes to grind were also involved in one way or another. Dawson may have cooked up the fraud with one of his colleagues, possibly Sir Arthur Keith of the Hunterian Museum, to get one over on their rivals. It's also quite possible that one of them, or perhaps a group of conspirators, played on Dawson's ambition to discredit and humiliate him. In the murky underworld of palaeontologists, it's more difficult to unearth the truth than it is to find a prize fossil. So, who are the principal suspects, apart from the serial faker Dawson? Well, the list is long and, perhaps unsurprisingly, many of the people on it were Sussex residents.

It has been suggested that the whole thing was an elaborate joke by the local workmen employed on Dawson's excavation, but this doesn't really hold water: none of them would have known enough to produce credible fragments. They could, however, have been bribed to plant the evidence – and make sure that it was found.

An unlikely suspect, at first sight, was Dawson's distinguished neighbour in Crowborough, Sir Arthur Conan Doyle, creator of Sherlock Holmes but also author of *The Lost World*. Some say that he and Dawson were in it together, others that Doyle was working alone, and that his motive was to bring the scientific establishment into disrepute in the same way that he had been ridiculed for his advocacy of spiritualism and naïve belief in the spoof photos of the Cottingley Fairies. Conceivable, I suppose, but not really a clincher.

More likely are a couple of Hastings men, William Lewis Abbott and William Butterfield. Abbott knew Dawson well and was an amateur palaeontologist, too. He had the necessary knowledge, and may have wanted to arrange a prank at his friend's expense (strange sense of humour, palaeontologists). Butterfield, on the other hand, had a more sinister motive: as librarian at Hastings Museum, he was miffed when Dawson discovered an Iguanodon skeleton in Hastings and took it to the British Museum without telling him (particularly vengeful, librarians; look at Chairman Mao).

The British Museum connection throws up a few suspects too: Arthur Smith Woodward, Keeper of Geology, and Martin Hinton, a volunteer in Smith Woodward's department. They were both capable of the hoax – indeed, after Hinton's death, a trunk with his initials containing numerous forged artefacts was found at the museum – and as a friend of Dawson's, Woodward was one of the first to hear of the discovery and helped with later excavations and publicising the finds. Another friend of Dawson's, Samuel Woodhead of the Uckfield Agricultural College, was also implicated, allegedly in collaboration with John Hewitt, Professor of Chemistry at Queen Mary College, London – although what they stood to gain from the hoax is debatable. In fact, accusations were flung at just about everybody – even the French Jesuit priest Pierre Teilhard de Chardin, who assisted Dawson at Piltdown and discovered a crucial canine tooth.

But all the evidence points to Dawson, and really the only mystery is why it took so long to realise *Eoanthropus dawsoni*'s finder was a shameless charlatan. Doubts had been raised from the very beginning, but were soon dismissed because of the kudos of the find. Even when fluorine testing in 1950 dated the fossils as considerably less than four million years old, scientists adjusted their evolutionary theories to fit, and it wasn't until 1953 that the game was finally up. For 40 years, British palaeontologists ignored the mounting evidence against the veracity of Piltdown Man and skewed the facts to fit what they wanted to believe, that the 'missing link' was British, and moreover originated in Sussex.

More Salacious Detail

◈ At Barkham Manor (now the Barkham Manor Vineyard), Piltdown, there is a memorial stone you can visit. The inscription reads: 'Here in the old river gravel Mr Charles Dawson, FSA found the fossil skull of Piltdown Man, 1912-1913. The discovery was described by Mr Charles Dawson and Sir Arthur Smith Woodward in the Quarterly Journal of the Geological Society 1913-15.'

◈ The nearby pub was renamed The Piltdown Man in honour of the momentous discovery

SCAM BY THE SEASIDE

MR NEVILLE'S 'HOMES FIT FOR HEROES'

'A rash on the countryside.'

NIKLAUS PEVSNER

Peacehaven, that little strip of bungalow heaven, is coming up for its centenary; it had a dubious birth and bad press from the sniffy elite, but it's still there, its denizens love it, and it is a testament to one man's sincere desire to make a lot of money.

That man was Charles Neville, a cheery adventurer, entrepreneur and huckster who would probably have sold tickets to his grandmother's funeral but it would have been a grand show and it would not have-meant that he didn't love her. It was not his fault he had more front than Eastbourne. Huckstering was in his blood. He was the son of an exhibition promoter and grandson of a man who accompanied Napoleon to Elba on his first exile. Or so he claimed.

In 1914, Neville bought the land that is now Peacehaven from the Marquess of Abergavenny (whose name was, by amazing coincidence, William Nevill; surely Charles must have been able to parlay that it into some kind of advantage?). It cost him £15,000, and he was able to afford this kind of seed money as he had made quite a fortune in the colonies. Born in Darlington in 1881, he had gone first to Toronto (which had been too staid for him) then to Australia, where he'd bought a ship, the *Snark* (presumably impossible to hunt down), sailed off to New Guinea and negotiated lucrative mineral rights from one of the tribal chiefs. With brass safely in pocket he returned to Canada, where he bought up tracts of land, parcelled it up into bite-size pieces and sold it to British and European immigrants. You can see where this is going, can't you?

Obviously still finding Canada a bit dull, he returned to Rottingdean in 1912, married Dorothy and settled down; but he was still only 31, and he must have wanted something to fiddle with, and thought his Canadian scheme worth reviving. So he bought a lump of land and sub-divided it up into parcels 100 ft by 25 ft (30 m by 7 m). Realising that a strip of bare windswept mud with no amenities was not exactly a punter-magnet, and that if he wanted people to come, he would have to build it, he made a huge splash to put the place on the map by launching a nationwide competition to name the brave new world, with a cash prize for the winner and land parcels for the runners-up. PR was his métier. Maximum publicity, minimal outlay; 80,000 people entered; two people shared the £100 prize to name the place (New Anzac-on-Sea) but, and here comes the scam, 2,445 other people 'won' strips of land, which would be theirs for a conveyancing fee of £4. Do the maths, and you get a healthy profit of £9K or so. The *Daily Express* got all righteous, sued him for fraud and won. He had to pay back all the money, but the case had generated the kind of publicity you couldn't buy.

Living the dream proved more difficult. The winners who took up their land found their paradise consisted of wooden shacks, tar paper huts, tents, mud, filth and grazing animals, no clean water, sewerage, transport or power. There was also a war on, and materials (and people to use them) were in short supply. It took a certain pioneering spirit to stick it out. Many didn't take up their land, or sold it to others, and to this day there is some residual confusion and legal wrangling about who owns what land. In short, a mess. But was Neville downhearted? No. The Bounceback Factor was strong in the DNA. When the war finished in 1918 he had quietly renamed it Peacehaven, and started to market it as a place where 'homes fit for heroes' could be built. Ever the showman, he organised guided charabanc tours, sent out brochures full of 'artist's impressions' of what Peacehaven would look like when it grew up and even paid for the first ever glider display to get folks to roll up and see the show. Neville may have been 60 per cent snake-oil merchant, but his optimism won the day; the people did come, and electricity was eventually installed in 1924. Peacehaven grew: admittedly into the kind of ugly sprawl that gets aesthetic knickers in a twist, and not quite the verdant Garden City it was sold as, but a real place.

More Salacious Detail

◉ *In Graham Greene's Brighton Rock, Peacehaven was where Pinkie Brown intended to murder Rose by throwing her off the cliff*

THE NAPOLEON OF FINANCE

HORATIO BOTTOMLEY 1860-1933

'Then welcome home to Bottomley, Deny it if you can,
He played his part; he's right at heart, And every inch a man.'

MUSIC HALL SONG

In July 1927 the villagers of Upper Dicker put out the flags and hired the Hailsham Prize Band to prepare a hero's welcome for one of their own. The hero in question was Horatio Bottomley, returning home after a five-year stretch in prison for 'fraudulently converting to his own use sums of money entrusted to him by members of the public'.

The British seem to have a soft spot for a genial swindler. Bottomley did not let them down; he charmed and defrauded on an entertainingly Napoleonic scale, foreshadowing newspaper magnate Robert Maxwell and author-politician Jeffrey Archer. He must have had charisma by the bucket-load; people adored him, and queued up for the privilege of being swindled by a master. One anonymous fraud victim, fleeced of £40,000, a huge sum at the time, and not to be sneezed at today, stood up stoutly for him, despite bleeding heavily from the wallet. For him:

> *Anyone who says a word against Bottomley I will quarrel with.*
> *I am not sorry I lent him the money, and I would do it again.*

The rise & rise of Horatio

During a spectacularly notorious career, Bottomley was a journalist, politician, womaniser, financial speculator and downright con man, often all at once. His biography reads like the synopsis of one of Dickens's lesser works. Even his name has a Pickwickian gloss. In true three-volume novel fashion, he started out ever so humble. Born in Bethnal Green in 1860, he lived in poverty with his parents until he was four years old, when they died, and he was placed in a Birmingham orphanage. When he was 14 he ran away to London to make his fortune at everyone else's expense. He started out as an errand boy in a law firm, then worked as a court reporter. In 1880 he married Eliza Norton, a respectable debt-collector's daughter from Battersea, and they settled in Clapham, where

Bottomley became a staunch and high-profile member of the Methodist church, at least in public, and they produced a daughter, Florence. The family man embarked on a life of audacious wheeling and dealing and managed to raise enough capital (don't ask how) to launch a small weekly periodical the *Hackney Hansard* in 1884. By manipulating advertising to raise capital, he acquired other journals and in 1889 he floated the Hansard Publishing Union on the stock exchange. It was a great success, but despite raising huge sums of money, two years later he was bankrupt and in court facing charges of fraud. The case caused a stir, not least because Bottomley defended himself, brilliantly, and was acquitted, leading some to comment that he could have had a fine legal career.

Mining for gold

However, a fine illegal career was more his forte; over the next few years, launching a joint stock trust, he invited the public to invest in West Australian mining companies. One was called Nil Desperandum. Money poured in; some found its way to the shareholders' pockets, but most ended up in Bottomley's. Between 1901 and 1905, no fewer than 67 writs and bankruptcy petitions were thrown at him, but the good ship Bottomley cruised through the choppy waters, acquiring money without apparent effort. The *Financial Times*, of which he was now chairman, described him as a 'man of millions' and with his newly acquired wealth – estimated at about £3 million – he built a country mansion, The Dicker, near Eastbourne. His lavish spending and genial character endeared him to the locals, who regarded him as their jovial squire: he threw wonderful parties, gave generously to the local cricket club, of which he was president, built splendid estate cottages for his workers and bred racehorses – he loved to gamble. Money went out as fast as it came in. Bottomley kept a luxury apartment in London's Pall Mall and, having packed his wife off to Monte Carlo, spent wildly on champagne, restaurants, theatre trips and a string of mistresses.

A brilliant public speaker with a massive ego, and an unstoppable urge to show off and fool all of the people most of the time, Bottomley was naturally drawn to politics. After two unsuccessful attempts, he was elected Liberal MP for South Hackney in 1906. That same year he launched the *John Bull* magazine (specialising in 'spicy' reports of murders and divorces and in the merciless exposure of 'vice and graft') ostensibly with the aim of speaking up for the 'common man' but actually for his own ends. He used the journal for rigged lotteries, competitions and sweepstakes, pocketing the proceeds and shamelessly promoting himself. *The Sunday Pictorial*, a popular right-wing organ for the masses at the time, contracted him to write articles for them at an astounding £100 a pop. I suppose he was an early celebrity columnist. Of course, he didn't actually write the articles – he subbed them out to others at a quarter of the fee and put his name on the end result. Not so much fraud as judicious brand management, you might argue. Even so, every now and then his lavish spending and fraudulence caught up with him. In 1909 he was charged with fraud but acquitted and in 1912 was declared bankrupt, again. He also lost his seat.

Bottomley needs you!

When war broke out in 1914 Bottomley instantly grasped its manifold money-making advantages, declared himself a reformed character and threw himself into a new role as 'the country's recruiting sergeant'. (He was, of course, far too old to serve himself.) He made rousing speeches, for which he charged a handsome fee, and turned the *John Bull* into a jingoistic mouthpiece. After one of his blood-stirring speeches at Hull, 1,000 men rushed off to enlist. By now a national hero, he regained his parliamentary seat, this time as an independent.

However, nemesis finally caught up with him. It all fell apart in 1919 when he launched a Victory Bond Club, inviting *John Bull* readers to invest in government victory bonds. At least £900,000 was raised and although some investors were paid, the organisation was chaotic and there were colossal losses; Bottomley himself was siphoning off thousands. In 1922 he ended up in court on charges of fraud. Again he conducted his own defence but despite protesting his innocence, and breaking down in tears, his silver tongue failed him, he was found guilty on all but one of the counts, and sentenced to seven years' imprisonment. He was also expelled from Parliament. His supporters and friends in Upper Dicker were stunned: as was Bottomley, who had so confidently assumed that he would slide out of trouble once again that he had bought tickets for a day at the races at Epsom.

Prison life in Wormwood Scrubs was hard for one so used to the good life, especially one who was too short and stout to fit into the prison uniform, but he maintained his wit. It is said that the prison chaplain on seeing Bottomley sewing mailbags, commented: 'Ah, sewing?' 'No,' replied Bottomley, 'reaping.' With good behaviour, he was released after five years. He returned to a warm welcome at Upper Dicker but never regained his former success. He made an effort, launching a new magazine, *John Blunt* in 1928, but it failed to grab the public imagination. His wife died in 1930 and he sold The Dicker to pay debts. A shadow of his former oratorical self, he took to the music hall stage to tell his life story to those who would pay to hear it. His favourite mistress, Peggy Primrose, a former chorus girl, took care of him but he died in 1933, an impoverished and rather pathetic figure. His ashes were scattered on the Downlands Gallops above Alfriston.

More Salacious Detail

⊚ Bottomley's former Sussex home, The Dicker, and its stables now house St Bede's co-education day and boarding school

⊚ The Rise and Fall of Horatio Bottomley: The Biography of a Swindler, Alan Hyman (Cassell, 1972)

⊚ Horatio Bottomley: A Biography, Julian Symons (Cresset Press, 1955)

⊚ The Times newspaper online archives: between 1897-1933 Horatio Bottomley was featured in more than 450 news items and editorials

PART FOUR

MURDER

B ecause of the imperfectibility of human beings, murder has been with us since Cain started to get bothered that Abel was looking at him in a funny way. And Sussex, of course, has had its fair share of illegal killings. The task here was to decide which ones to include.

According to celebrated crime writer P.D. James, all murders are motivated by one of the L words: love, lust, loathing or lucre; of course, she meant all interesting murders. Although it could be argued that boring professional hits or gangland turf-war takeouts are motivated by lucre, they do not tickle the horror gland in a shame-fully delicious manner, so this section doesn't cover the vicious killings of the notorious racecourse razor gangs, or the opportunistic killings of cut-throat smugglers.

Remembering always that this is a salacious guide, I have concentrated on murders brought about by motives more fascinat-ing than mere greed: jealousy, obsession, lust, betrayal, fear and passion – not to mention satanic influence and the desire for fame – many of them reaching the kind of nationwide notoriety that a county can be proud of, if not in a particularly good way, and attracting the attention of the finest legal brains in the land.

And, just a thought here, but isn't it about time that blood-spattered Eastbourne stopped pretending to be respectable?

THE BUTCHER OF RYE

THE MISTAKEN MURDER OF ALLEN GREBELL

'Killed by the cruel stab of a sanguinary butcher.'

INSCRIPTION ON THE TOMBSTONE OF ALLEN GREBELL

Today Rye appears to be not much more than a rather oppressively quaint tourist trap and literary 'experience', but once upon a time it was inhabited by real, properly surly Sussex natives, who got drunk and dirty and spilled blood.

The most notorious murder was carried out by John Breeds, or Breads, the landlord of the Flushing Inn and a butcher by trade. Possibly because of easy access to hard liquor and red meat, he seemed to suffer what modern Rye natives would no doubt call 'anger issues'; he certainly resented the mayor of Rye, James Lamb, who had once, in his capacity as magistrate, fined Breeds for giving short measures. It probably didn't help that Lamb was extremely wealthy, his fortune coming from a successful brewing business, and that he was the owner of Lamb House, the finest residence in Rye. Both of Breeds's enterprises were slowly sinking and he had turned into a drink-sodden festering lump of grudge-laden resentment; he had also convinced himself, on no evidence whatsoever, that it was all Lamb's fault.

One windy night in March 1743, James Lamb's son, Lieutenant George Lamb, an excise officer, threw a party on board his ship, berthed by the Ypres Tower. He had invited his father to join him, but James was feeling unwell; he asked his brother-in-law, Allen Grebell to go along and have some fun in his stead. Grebell was more than pleased to join the party, but as it was a wild night, borrowed James's distinctive red mayoral cloak to keep him dry for the short walk to the ship.

A glamorous VIP shipboard party was an event bound to be gossiped about in a small town, and John Breeds found out about it. He knew that James Lamb had been invited, and that he would come back from the ship through the churchyard not far from the Flushing Inn. Tonight would be the night when Breeds would have his revenge. After a few hours' stiffening his sinews with alcohol, Breeds armed himself with one of his butcher's knives, and went to the churchyard to lurk in wait for the author of all his misfortunes. Some time after midnight, a red-cloaked figure lurched merrily into the churchyard. Breeds seized his chance, leapt out from behind a gravestone and plunged the knife through the red cloak and into what he thought was James Lamb's body.

The outcome lacked drama. Grebell, well lubricated from the party, did not feel the blow, probably thought he had just collided with a fellow reveller and staggered off uncomplaining to his home. He sent his servant to bed, settled down in front the fire to sleep it off, and bled to death in the night, painlessly, we hope.

When he was discovered in the morning, the Rye justices did not have to exercise their detective skills overmuch to find his killer. John Breeds had spent much of the night running around the town, shouting 'Butchers Should Kill Lambs!' And his blood-stained knife – which had his name carved on the handle – was found where he had dropped it in the churchyard. Imagine his horror when he came up before the very man he thought he had despatched, the multitasking Mayor (and also Judge) James Lamb. No one questioned the legality of having the intended murder victim presiding over the trial of his intended murderer.

Breeds pleaded insanity, but it didn't wash; he was found guilty and sentenced to death. On a warm June day, he exercised a condemned man's privilege by downing his last drink at the Flushing Inn and was hanged outside the Strand Gate. His body was left to rot in a gibbet cage, a grisly deterrent to other would-be murderers. After 20 years, his bones were buried in St Mary's churchyard, but were mysteriously stolen. You can still see the top of his skull, if you really want to, hanging in its own iron cage in the Town Hall. It's a bracing antidote to all those cream teas and bijou art galleries.

More Salacious Detail

- Rye Town Hall, Market Street, Rye, East Sussex TN31 7LA.
  Website: www.ryetowncouncil.gov.uk
- Murder by Mistake, Kenneth Clark, available from Rye Museum.
  Website: www.ryemuseum.co.uk/MuseumSales.htm

A LEWES LOVE TRIANGLE

THE MURDER OF WILLIAM MOORE

'Have mercy upon me, O God, according to thy loving kindness'

PSALM 51

This is a sad tale of love, betrayal, murder and suicide. It all took place in Lewes in 1679, when England was still fairly merrie, as Charles II was on the throne, but nearly everything we know about it comes from a rather pious and patronising pamphlet (*A Warning to Young Men, or A Man of Bloods*) written in 1860, when Victorian values reigned supreme.

Robert Brinkhurst, 'tall, sulky and plump', was a 29-year-old cutler; William Moore, seven years his junior, was a handsome, apple-cheeked young draper's assistant whose halitosis was his downfall. Robert and William were inseparable; they lived the good life, eating and drinking 'to some measure of excess', and looting the neighbours' gardens for flowers. When they had to go to their separate homes at night, whoever woke up first would immediately open his window so that the other would know he was ready for the day. The pamphlet has some finger-wagging tut-tuttery about this mild debauchery:

> This friendship 'was not so good as great, for though it may be hoped they were not confederate, in many of those grand evils in which multitudes of young men are immersed; yet it may be feared there was too much time misspent.'

What the 'grand evils' might be is not explained; think your worst.

Into this idyllic friendship there slid a snake. In 1678, a suave, seditious, tricksy Londoner arrived in Lewes to visit friends. He was called John Newton, and he was looking for some lazy fun to while away a long idle summer. Poor William was bedazzled by Newton's metropolitan charm, drawn into an intimacy with the glamorous townee, leaving lumpy, unsophisticated Robert out in the cold.

Like all holiday romances, this one faded. John Newton went back to the bright lights, and William and Robert were friends again. William must have thought he was forgiven and it was forgotten; Robert, however, festered in silence, evolving a truly vindictive revenge. It took him a long time.

Over a year later, in November 1679, he had a letter sent from London to William; it was supposed to come from Newton and contained a packet of yellow powder to cure William's chronic bad breath. It doesn't bear thinking about, does it? Poor William, no doubt flattered that his London friend had thought of him and was trying to help his embarrassing personal problem, eagerly swallowed the powder. It was arsenic. It took William several days to die, vomiting all the while, with Robert at his side.

No suspicion fell on Robert, but he was in his own hell.

> '[He] had no quiet in his mind; he enjoyed not himself in the daytime, nor
> cared to lye alone in the night. Nor could one mention Mr Moore to him, but
> he was ready to break forth into tears.'

Two weeks later, the wretched Robert's plot was revealed, probably to his great relief. He was arrested and hauled before a Justice of the Peace at the Turk's Head Tavern. When shown a sample of yellow arsenic for identification, he grabbed it and stuffed it in his mouth. Sure enough, a few days later, he died, in some agony, to the sound of Psalm 51.

What followed was even worse. Despite a petition by his family, Robert, as both a murderer and a suicide, was denied a Christian burial. His corpse was bundled up in a shroud that showed his face and feet, thrown on a dung cart and paraded through the town. He was buried in a shallow grave at the crossroads where Lewes Prison now stands; a crossroads is where the devil hangs out, ready to snap up lost souls. As if that wasn't enough, a stake was plunged through his bowels and left sticking up above the earth, presumably as a warning to others. It's said that the local children used the stake for Maypole games for some years afterwards, so it must have been quite a size.

More Salacious Detail

◈ A Warning to Young Men or A Man of Bloods *was formerly held in a single copy in the library of the Rt Honourable Thomas Grenville, but is now at the British Library*

EXCESS BAGGAGE

THE BRIGHTON TRUNK MURDERS

'A hand-bag?'

OSCAR WILDE, *THE IMPORTANCE OF BEING EARNEST*

Perhaps it is Brighton's status as a railway terminus that encourages this sort of thing, but it has seen more than its fair share of bodies stuffed into trunks. In 1934, there were two of them, and unkind persons nicknamed the town the Queen of Slaughtering Places.

On June 17th, cloakroom attendant William Joseph Vinnicombe noticed a terrible stench coming from a plywood trunk that had lain unclaimed at the left luggage office for 11 days. When the railway police opened it, they found a female torso and arms parcelled up in brown paper. Other mainline stations were alerted and the next day another trunk was discovered at King's Cross Station in London containing the legs and feet of the very same victim.

Trunk murder No. 1

A post-mortem revealed that the woman, around 25, had been pregnant when she died, but no cause of death could be established. Brighton's Chief Constable called in Scotland Yard and there was a direct nationwide appeal for help through the press – the first time the police had used this method. Lists of missing young women, a description of the victim ('well-nourished, about 5 feet 2 inches tall') and photographs of the trunk were circulated throughout the country; thousands of statements were taken and people wrote in their hundreds with sightings or clues. Despite this constabulary frenzy, neither the woman nor her murderer has ever been identified.

A totally unsubstantiated but very salacious local legend has it that the woman had been an accidental victim of a botched job by Hove abortionist Dr Edward Massiah. He was questioned, but never charged; he was supposed to have done too many favours for too many big cheeses (including royalty) who moved together to close down any police action.

However, one thing that did come out of the high-profile publicity campaign and door-to-door search for information about Trunk Murder No. 1 was the discovery of Trunk Murder No. 2...

The death of Violette Kaye

In response to the call for information about missing young women, the local press in Brighton received a tip-off that a Miss Violette (or Violet) Kaye (or Saunders) was missing, and passed it on to the police. After that it all got a bit Graham Greene. Violette Kaye was a music hall dancer and prostitute, and had not been seen walking her regular beat for some days. She lived a volatile life with her young lover, Tony Mancini, 26, and on May 10th there had been an ugly scene at the Skylark Café on the seafront, where he worked, when Violette had caught him flirting with one of the teenage waitresses. No one had seen her since. Mancini told friends that she had gone to Paris on a dancing job and given some of her clothes to the flirty young waitress. He also moved out of the lodgings they had shared at 44 Park Crescent.

When Violette's name came to their attention, the police pulled in Tony Mancini (aka John Notyre, Tony English, Hyman Gold and Cecil Lois England, his actual name) as a matter of course; as a small time crook, he was used to helping police with their enquiries, although they (the police) were probably not that hopeful, as Violette was at least 15 years older than the victim in Trunk No. 1. Mancini was released after questioning and immediately did a runner to London.

At first he was not missed. However, on July 15th during a routine house-to-house search, still in pursuit of clues to the Trunk Murder No.1, the police called at 52 Kemp Street, Mancini's new address, where a foul stench led them to his basement room. There they found a black trunk at the end of the bed, covered with a cloth and doing service as a coffee table, despite the smell and the leaking bodily fluids. Apparently Mancini's landlady, Mrs Barnard, had no sense of smell. When they opened it, they found the body (entire) of Violette Kaye, killed by a blow to the head. A warrant went out, and Mancini was arrested on July 17th in Lee, south-east London.

To have one trunk murder in your town is a tragedy; to have two looks like a serial killer; but in this case it wasn't, there was nothing to link the two killings. Mancini was tried in December 1934 at Lewes Assizes, under the name of John Notyre in case you want to look it up. The trial lasted five days. You would have thought it an open and shut case: the accused was the victim's lover with whom she had had a public quarrel; the body had been found in a trunk at the end of his bed; it was proved that Mancini had sent a telegram to Violette's sister saying that she had gone to France when she hadn't; Violette's friends testified that they had heard him claiming that he had given his 'missus' the biggest hiding of her life. Short of being caught by all 12 jurors beating poor Violette over the head with a hammer, what else do you want? Well obviously a lot more, as Mancini got off.

Getting away with it

Mancini's defence was that he had come back and found Violette dead in their lodgings in Park Crescent. Afraid that his criminal record would count against him, your honour, he had simply panicked, stuffed her body in a trunk and wheeled it to his new room in Kemp Street, then entered into a state of denial. There was also some nitpickery over the forensic evidence; and Norman Birkett, KC, for the defence, sowed the seeds of reasonable doubt in the jury's collective mind in the traditional manner by shifting the blame on to the victim, pointing out that Violette could have been killed by a client (because, after all, she was a prostitute, and so deserved all she got) or fallen down the stairs (because, after all, she was also a drinker, so deserved all she got). The jury was out for two and a half hours. Amazingly they came back with a verdict of not guilty. Mancini could not believe it; neither could the judge.

Decades later, when the death penalty was no longer in force, Mancini confessed to the killing. In 1976 he told the *News of the World* that he had killed Violette during a raging row. She had attacked him with the coal hammer, he had wrested it from her, but then threw it at her when she demanded it back. It hit her on the left temple, and killed her. We'll never really know.

The very first trunk murder

The sensational trunk murders of the summer of 1934 inspired the gutter press to dig deeper for more dirt, and sure enough they came up with the original Brighton trunk murder, which had taken place just over a century previously.

The murderer, John Holloway, did not have such a smart defence lawyer as Mancini, and was hanged in Lewes in 1831 for the murder of his first wife, Celia. It's a very sad tale. He was a respectable boy, brought up in Litlington by his grandparents, who taught him to read and write and encouraged him to become an active member of the Alfriston Baptist Chapel. Then Mammon struck, the Holloways all moved to Brighton to find work. It was 1818, Brighton was rocking under the rule of Prinny (*see p. 12-15*). John fell into a dissolute life of petty crime, heavy drinking and much mollocking.

When he was 18, he met Celia Bashford, six years older than him, who was in service in Brighton. She fell in love with him, but not he with her, although that did not stop him enjoying her favours. When she became pregnant, he refused to marry her, so she went home to Ardingly and applied for parish relief. The Poor Law Authorities leaned heavily on John and he was imprisoned for five weeks until he agreed to marry her. The child was stillborn and the shaky marriage collapsed.

Holloway joined the Naval Reserve, took up with other women and eventually, and bigamously, married Ann Kennett in Rye. When the couple returned to Brighton looking for work, the law slapped a maintenance order on him to support Celia. Promising that they would get back together, he lured her to their 'new' lodging, where he strangled her with the help of Ann Kennett. They burnt her clothes, dismembered her body, threw the head and limbs into the privy, stuffed the torso in a trunk and wheeled it in a barrow up to Lovers Lane in Preston Village, where they buried it in a shallow grave. It was discovered a week later when rain washed the soil away.

More Salacious Detail

◗ *There is a Victorian plaque dedicated to Celia Holloway in St John's Churchyard; the details are wrong but the sentiment is true; 52 Kemp Street still stands, as does 44 Park Crescent*

CREEPY CRAWLEY

THE ACID BATH MURDERER

'If I told you the truth you wouldn't believe me.
It sounds too fantastic for belief.'

JOHN GEORGE HAIGH

The Acid Bath Murders were the sensation of Britain in the late 1940s: serial killings high on the yuk factor, with a juicy frisson of the macabre. The perpetrator, John George Haigh, was a mediocre fraudster, fantasist, smooth-talking con artist, serial jailbird and sociopath. He also claimed that he drank the blood of his victims, but this was probably a bid to set up an insanity plea just in case he was found guilty. What he did, he did for the money. And where did he perpetrate these foul deeds? Crawley, the pride of the brave new post-war world. It certainly put the fledgling new town on the map, for all the wrong reasons.

Haigh had already killed and rendered into sludge five victims and forged their signatures to get at their cash, property and assets before he was caught in 1949, after doing the same to 69-year-old Mrs Olive Durand-Deacon, a widow of substantial means. He had met her at the Onslow Court Hotel, Kensington, where he had been living on his ill-gotten gains and posing as an entrepreneurial engineer while looking for easy pickings. Mrs Durand-Duncan had an entrepreneurial streak herself, and she suggested a plan for manufacturing false nails. On February 18th, Haigh invited her down to see his 'factory', Hurstlea Products, at Leopold Road, West Green in Crawley. It was nothing but a lock-up, but Mrs Durand-Deacon did not have time to show any surprise, as Haigh shot her in the back of the head with the .38 Enfield revolver he had stolen from one of his previous victims, stripped her of her jewellery and the Persian lamb coat she wore, and stuffed her body in a 40-gallon tank. After a refreshing cup of tea and light snack at the café across the street, Haigh came back to pump concentrated sulphuric acid into the tank to cover the body, then went to dine at the George Hotel.

A successful formula

He knew exactly what to do, and how long the body would take to dissolve, as he had done this before. Assigned to the prison workshop during one of his stretches, he had discovered how easy it was to dissolve a body (a mouse) in sulphuric acid. He thought he had hit upon the way to commit the perfect murder. Fresh out of gaol for the third time in 1944, he had bumped into wealthy William McSwan for whom he had once worked as a chauffeur. McSwan was the perfect unsuspecting victim, so pleased to see the plausible Haigh that he introduced him to his parents. By early September, McSwan's body was dissolving slowly in a drum of acid in Haigh's basement at 79 Gloucester Road, Kensington, and his assets being siphoned off into Haigh's pockets.

He moved into McSwan's house, telling his parents that William had fled to Scotland to avoid being called up for war service. In July 1945, when McSwan's money ran out, and his parents were wondering why he hadn't come back from exile and started asking questions, Haigh did the same to them, stole their pension cheques, forged their signatures, sold their properties and moved into the Onslow Court Hotel.

In 1947, possibly thinking that an industrial space would be more suitable for his burgeoning business, Haigh relocated his acid bath to Crawley and found two new victims, Dr Archibald Henderson and his wife Rose, to re-capitalise his enterprise. The Hendersons were selling a house, and advertised the fact in the local paper. Haigh went to view it. He killed them both on February 12th 1948, using the doctor's own revolver which he had stolen on his recce visit, then forged papers allowing him to sell all their possessions. He kept their dog. A year later, he found his next, and final, victim.

A bath too far

After three days and some judicious topping up, Haigh considered that Mrs Durand-Deacon's body had been 'disappeared' safely, and so he drained out the sludge into the workshop yard. But Mrs Durand-Deacon, a woman of strict routine, had friends, and she had been missed. Constance Lane reported her missing, and so did Haigh himself, who claimed she had missed an appointment with him; he was extremely keen to help police with their enquiries. (This is called hubris.) Meanwhile, he took the Persian lamb coat to the dry cleaners and sold the jewellery to Mr Bull the pawnbroker in Horsham for £100, leaving a trail of paper evidence that would come back and haunt him.

It was in Horsham that his past caught up with him. Because he had been so officious and keen about helping the police, they looked into his background. His criminal record was examined closely, particularly the charges for fraud and theft, and it was easy for the police to get a warrant to search the workshop. As well as three 10-gallon glass bottles – two containing acid – rubber boots, rubber gloves, and a gas mask, they found the dry cleaner's receipt for Mrs Durand-Deacon's coat, a marriage certificate, passports, identity cards, drivers' licences relating to the Hendersons and the McSwan family, and a recently fired .38 Enfield revolver, with ammunition, packed away in a hat box. In the grisly sludge in the workshop yard, pathologist Dr Keith Simpson found three gallstones, the remains of a human foot, a set of custom-made false teeth, a red plastic bag handle, and a lipstick container. Haigh was arrested on February 28th and remanded in Horsham Police Station.

'How can you prove murder without a body?'

After some inspired but unconvincing fabrication, Haigh confessed. It appears that he had woefully misunderstood the term '*habeas corpus*'; he believed that if there were no body to be found, there could be no conviction of murder, not even if he confessed. When disabused of this notion, he switched to his back-up plan. He explained in gory detail how he had killed his victims, but that the motive had not been to take their money but to drink their blood. It was not his fault, he had a mental condition. He suffered from an overwhelming compulsion to drink blood, a compulsion preceded by blood-drenched dreams; plus he heard the voices that told him to kill. He also claimed to have killed a nameless girl from Eastbourne, a woman in Hammersmith and a young man called Max from Kensington, although these deaths were never substantiated. Clearly he was going for the Broadmoor option.

The case was notorious, especially the blood drinking aspect, blown up out of all proportion by the likes of the *Daily Mirror*, who labelled Haigh 'the vampire killer'. The Attorney-General himself, Sir Hartley Shawcross KC, led for the prosecution at Lewes Assizes when the trial opened on July 18th 1949. The defence, led by Maxwell Fyfe, went for the insanity plea, and wheeled out a battery of mental experts. Haigh appeared to have bedazzled quite a few of them, but then he did have a friend at Sussex Psychiatric Hospital from whom he learned what was needed to appear a couple of sandwiches short of a picnic, and he was a plausible and accomplished con artist. The jury was having none of it, and took under half an hour to come back with a verdict of plain old guilty on July 19th. The trial lasted just one day, which must have disappointed the legal teams. Haigh was sentenced to death.

While awaiting his death in Wandsworth Prison, he was examined again by three doctors to make absolutely sure he was sane and criminal, rather than criminally insane. They decided he'd known exactly what he was doing, and there was no reprieve. He went out on what I am sure he would have thought a high note, finally achieving the fame and notoriety he felt he deserved, as he was hanged at Wandsworth on August 10th by England's Chief Executioner, Albert Pierrepoint. He bequeathed his clothing to Madame Tussaud's Chamber of Horrors.

More Salacious Detail

⟩ *At Horsham Museum you can see Haigh's comb, prison card, signature, the door to the cell he was kept in at Horsham Police Station and a bizarre letter from a Mr Sherriff (25) writing to ask if he could use Haigh's car (a rather racy Alvis) 'until he needed it again'. Horsham Museum, 9 Causeway, Horsham RH12 1HE. Website: www.horshammuseum.org*

DEATH BY CHOCOLATE

THE MURDER OF SIDNEY ALBERT BARKER

'Like the measles, love is most dangerous when it comes late in life.'

LORD BYRON

This is a tale of obsessive lust, self-delusion, stalking, strychnine, chocolate and a very sad little death. It started with a glance, when eyes met on the Brighton seafront, and ended up such a *cause-célèbre* that the trial was moved from Lewes to London's Old Bailey.

In 1870, 42-year-old Christiana Edmunds moved with her widowed mother from Margate to Brighton. It was while Miss Edmunds was strolling along the prom that her eyes chanced to meet those of Arthur Beard, a local doctor of unblemished reputation. She imagined she saw lustful appreciation and undying love in the doctor's eyes; you know how it is with women of a certain age and the medical profession.

She found out his name and where he lived, and then she bombarded him with passionate love letters, in Italian. Dr Beard made the fatal mistake of being kind to her, rather than taking out an injunction, so Christiana continued in her deluded obsession. All that stood in the way of her eternal happiness was the inconvenient Mrs Beard. She hatched a terrible plan to get rid of her rival.

Claiming that she had to deal with 'some troublesome cats', she bought strychnine from chemist Isaac Garrett in Queen's Road, and injected it into a batch of chocolate creams. Then she called on Mrs Beard, and sweetly pressed a chocolate on her; Mrs Beard spat it out because it tasted foul. Christiana stormed off, taking her chocolates (the evidence) with her. Once again, Dr Beard failed to seize the moment, did not go to the police, but told Miss Edmunds that he suspected her of trying to poison his wife and never to darken his door again.

Outraged, she accused him of slander, then set about proving that she was innocent by the simple strategy of randomly poisoning every-body else in Brighton. She bribed various children to buy chocolates from J.G. Maynard, a confectioner in West Street; then she doctored them with arsenic and strychnine, and sent them back to be exchanged on some pretext. Maynard's shelves gradually filled up with lethal little treats. Over the next few weeks, several people fell seriously ill and Maynard's reputation was impugned, but it wasn't until June 1871, when poor little Sidney Albert Barker, aged four, died after eating one of the chocolates that things started to go really wrong.

Christiana was counting on the child's death to lead to Maynard's arrest, so that she would be in the clear; but the inquest, at which she testified falsely against Maynard, returned a verdict of accidental death. There was outrage in the town, with Christiana leading the charge at full vigilante tilt. She berated the police for not doing their job properly; she even wrote three anonymous letters to Sidney's father, urging him to take action against Maynard, accusing him of letting down his child.

Nothing happened, so Christiana decided to ratchet up the alarm and despondency, particularly among Brighton's sweet of tooth. Anonymous parcels of poisoned pastries and fruit were sent to various town worthies; she cleverly included herself in the distribution. People fell ill. She chivvied the police even more, until they offered a reward; and that was her downfall. Garrett the chemist suddenly remembered her poison purchases; the children she had bribed came forward; Dr Beard took her Italian billets-doux to the police, who discovered that they matched the writing on the anonymous letters to Mr Barker. In December 1871 Christiana was arrested, charged with the murder of Sidney Barker and the attempted murder of Mrs Beard. She claimed wildly that she was pregnant by Dr Beard, which of course she wasn't, The trial opened at the Central Criminal Court in January 1872. Christiana was found guilty and sentenced to death.

All Brighton was thrilled, but the nation felt bad about condemning a middle-class gentlewomen to the noose, and on appeal Edmunds was sent to Broadmoor, where she stayed until her death, aged 78.

More Salcious Detail

❂ *The Edmunds residence still stands at 16 Gloucester Place, Brighton*

❂ The Great Chocolate Murders, *a play by John Fletcher,*
was broadcast on March 4th 2006 on Radio 4

THE FATAL ONION PIE

THE MURDER OF WILLIAM FRENCH

'Indeed the tears live in an onion that should water this sorrow.'

WILLIAM SHAKESPEARE, *ANTHONY AND CLEOPATRA, ACT I, SCENE II*

On Saturday April 10th 1852, Sarah Ann French had the distinction of being the last woman to be hanged in Sussex. She had been found guilty of murdering her husband by lacing his Christmas Eve onion pie with arsenic.

William French, a 35-year-old farm labourer from Chiddingly, had complained of stomach pains on Christmas Eve, retched and heaved his way over the Christmas holidays, had a few days' remittance, and then succumbed to a very unpleasant death just after midnight on January 7th. An inquest was held at the Gun Inn at Chiddingly and, on the evidence of Henry Holman, surgeon, the jury decided that poor William French had died from natural causes.

However, village gossip being village gossip, the inquest was soon re-opened, convening at the Six Bells; the grieving widow had been so distraught she had taken strapping young labourer James Hickman to her bed for some comfort on the day of the funeral, and her sister had come too. On February 2nd, Sarah French found herself charged with the wilful murder of her husband. The trial would be at Lewes.

Sarah French was a kind of rustic, illiterate Mrs Robinson. Apparently happily married to Mr French, her fancy had been tickled by James Hickman, only 20 at the time, and her sister's beau. That relationship was soon over, but James was still welcomed at the French home, rather reluctantly on William's part, because unlike his hosts, he could read and write, and used to read bedtime stories to their little boy. Sarah flirted outrageously with James, inviting herself to sit on his knee, kissing him, giving him a silver ring 'to remember her by', telling him casually of immense wealth (£500) that she had hidden away, and asking (expecting the answer yes) if he would like to go to bed with her if her husband were no longer an obstacle.

More or less everyone in Chiddingly seems to have testified at the trial, and there was a mass of confusing evidence about who bought how much arsenic where, when and from whom. Dr Alfred Swain Taylor, professor of medical jurisprudence and chemistry at Guy's Hospital was brought in, made mincemeat of Henry Holman and proved that William French's corpse contained at least 11 grains of arsenic, four times more than the killing dose. Although it could not be proved, as there was none of it left to examine, it was probably the onion pie – the 'rarity' that Sarah cooked specially for William on Christmas Eve – wot done it. Sarah herself had put the blame on the pie when William fell ill, although she took care not to call in a doctor who could have settled the matter once and for all.

As the trial progressed, and it became apparent that things were going against her, Sarah issued a desperate statement from her cell hoping to push the blame on to her toy boy; she claimed that it had been Hickman all the time, he had slipped the arsenic into the pie and had promised to marry her if she did not tell on him.

The jury was having none of this, and it only took them an hour to find her guilty. On March 27th she was sentenced to death. After her hanging, which was so well attended that a roadblock had to be set up across North Street to prevent carriage gridlock, Sarah French was buried in a lead-lined coffin in the grounds of the town gaol (which stood in North Street at the time). The case was much reported in the press, and prompted a debate about the efficacy of hanging as a deterrent: apparently, three years earlier, Sarah had gone to Lewes, with William, to witness the execution of Mary Ann Gearing from Guestling, hanged for poisoning her husband and children. Apparently, she had learned nothing from this grim event.

More Salacious Detail

⊙ The ghost of Sarah French has, allegedly, been seen at the Six Bells, Chiddingly, because the jury sat in the top bar while considering their verdict; but then, it is a pub. Apparently in the 1980s, it featured onion pie on the menu, without irony

⊙ For a transcription of the extremely detailed newspaper reports of the time, go to the Sussex Online Parish Clerks at www.sussex-opc.org

DEATH IN A BUNGALOW

THE MURDER OF EMILY KAYE

'See how love and murder will out.'

WILLIAM CONGREVE, *THE DOUBLE DEALER,* 1694

Only four years after the murder of Irene Munro (*see p.75*), had rocked the gentility of Eastbourne, the town was once again shocked by an even more ghastly murder in more or less the same place. It was so horrific that entrepreneurs were forced to set up booths round the site to sell tickets and refreshments to the prurient, who came in their coachloads to be shocked and disgusted.

Dashing womaniser, bank robber, fraudster and all-round irresistible Irish charmer, Patrick Herbert Mahon believed that he could get away with murder; and he would have done if his wife had not found a left-luggage ticket in his suit pocket.

This charming man

In the spring of 1924, Mahon, a sweet-talking salesman from Kew in London, came across 30-something Emily Kaye, a secretary in a City accountancy firm. He switched on the charm, she fell for it, and pretty soon he was promising her everything and she believed he would leave his wife and child for her; he even bought her a diamond and sapphire ring, probably with her own money, as he fleeced her mercilessly for her £600 savings. Then she discovered she was pregnant. Mahon, who had only been in it for the craic and the money, had to find a way out.

Using an assumed name (of course), he rented a cosy love nest, a former coastguard bungalow on the Crumbles; it even had roses round the door. He promised Emily that they would go to South Africa together to start a new life. She told all her friends, gave up her London flat and on April 7th moved down to the south coast. Eight days later, she was dead.

Mahon brought Emily's travel trunk to the cottage on April 11th, and then went back to London, ostensibly to get a passport. While there, he stayed in his own home at Kew with his wife, and honed his flirting skills by picking up a young woman, Ethel Duncan, while out walking in Richmond, and arranging a date with her. He also purchased a tenon saw and a cook's knife.

At his trial he claimed, sobbing all the while, that he and Emily had quarrelled, that she had attacked him and had fallen and hit her head, and after that he had panicked and it had all gone blank, your honour. What actually happened was that on April 15th, he had killed Emily, locked her body in the spare room and gone to bed. Next day he went up to London, dined with silly Ethel Duncan, and invited her down to the cottage for the Easter weekend.

Good Friday (April 18th) saw him dismembering Emily's body, and stowing the parts in her own trunk. When Ethel arrived at the bungalow, she saw the trunk but thought nothing of it, nor did she think it odd of him to start nailing up the spare room door in her presence. You have to wonder quite what she did notice. When Ethel had gone, Mahon spent the week disposing of the body parts. He burnt the head, feet and arms in the fire grate, packed the heart and messy organs in a biscuit tin, boiled up the torso and cut it up into bite-size pieces, and put as many of these as he could in his Gladstone bag, so that he could throw them out of the carriage window on his train journey to Waterloo.

A ticket to eternity

If he had not put the bag into left luggage (he was planning a return trip for the rest of the bits that were still in the trunk), and kept the ticket in his suit pocket, he would not have been caught; Emily's friends thought she was in South Africa and there was nothing to connect Mr Mahon, salesman, with Mr Waller, tenant of the bungalow. But loyal little Mavourneen Mahon wasn't as dumb as he may have taken her for, and went up to Waterloo with a private detective, John Beard, to investigate what was in left luggage. And when the police discovered what was in the bag (blood-stained knife, torn silk bloomers, silk scarf and Emily's canvas racket bag, with her initials on) they put it back where they found it and lay in wait for Mahon to come and collect.

Of course he denied everything; he often carried dog meat in his bag, that would explain the blood. And he had no idea how the other things had got there. Finally, after ten hours interrogation, he confessed. Mahon was charged with Emily Kaye's murder at Hailsham, and attended the grisly inquest (at his own request) at the bungalow. Sir Bernard Spilsbury, the Home Office pathologist, had spent eight hours putting Emily Kaye's body back together again, as well as he could, and described it as the most gruesome case he had ever worked on. Her head was never found.

Mahon was sent to trial at Lewes on July 15th, and gave evidence for five hours, evidently hoping to blarney his way out of his predicament, and blaming Emily for leading him astray. And maybe he could have got away with manslaughter; but it did not help his case that he was exposed as a heartless philanderer with a wife and child in London, a mistress on the coast and a floozy in between. He was found guilty and hanged in September at Wandsworth Prison, London.

More Salacious Detail

◗ *It was after this grisly case that Sir Bernard Spilsbury introduced the standard scene-of-crime murder bags, and the compulsory wearing of rubber gloves for sifting through evidence*

A BODY ON THE BEACH

THE MURDER OF IRENE MUNRO

'Murder most foul'

WILLIAM SHAKESPEARE, *HAMLET, ACT I, SCENE V*

On August 20th 1920, 13-year-old William Weller and his mother were picnicking on the shingle of the Crumbles at Eastbourne. William wandered off in search of treasure, but soon came back; he had stumbled upon the body of a young woman laying in a scrape of pebbles, her face beaten beyond recognition. Not far from the body lay a blood spattered ironstone brick. When the news broke, Eastbourne was shocked to the respectable core.

Smart, self-possessed Irene Munro had been taking a holiday alone, having fun walking, enjoying the sight of Eastbourne's glamorous seaplane, and fitting in a little shopping. On the afternoon of August 19th, she had gone out for a walk along the Crumbles, and that was the last her landlady saw of her until she was obliged to identify the body in the morgue, recognisable only by Irene's bright green coat.

It did not take the police long to catch up with William Thomas Gray and Jack Alfred Field, the two young men who had been seen by many people walking and laughing with Irene. They were arrested on August 24th, gave spurious and easily disproved alibis, were re-arrested and jointly charged on September 4th with wilful murder. The trial took place at Lewes between December 13th and 18th. Evidence was circumstantial, but there was a lot of it. The jury took only an hour to find them guilty, recommending mercy as it was unpremeditated. The pair were sentenced to death, but appealed in January 1921. They ruined their chances by each accusing the other and contradicting their earlier evidence. The appeal failed and they were hanged on February 2nd.

More Salacious Detail

❯ *The case was a gift for what was then the tabloid press, and the* John Bull Magazine
*(prop. H. Bottomley, see p.50) funded the defence, retaining top silk Sir Edward Marshall Hall
to defend Gray*

SATAN IN LEWES

THE DEATH OF NICHOLAS GARGANI

'Talk of the Devil and his horns appear.'

SAMUEL TAYLOR COLERIDGE

On April 17th 1996, 26-year-old Nicholas Gargani, eco-worrier, environmental activist and prominent member of the Lewes reAction group (formed to oppose development on the Downs), plunged to his death from the cliffs just outside Lewes. At the inquest an open verdict was returned; it has never been determined whether he jumped, fell or was pushed, physically or psychologically.

The story has all the hallmarks of the 17th century, when witchfinder-generals stalked the land and there was not enough reality TV. The death took place at a time when Lewes was plagued by graveyard desecrations and the mutilation of animals, particularly cats, in what appeared to be a ritualistic manner. Hearsay, gossip, wild accusations and an hysterical atmosphere surrounded the investigation, and sometimes it seemed that Lewes was gearing itself up for *The Wicker Man 2*.

Nick Gargani's friends and family made it very clear that he had nothing to do with the black arts. The nearest he had come to it was ordering a few New Age books and candles online, which is practically compulsory behaviour in Lewes. Yet when police went to his home, they found the walls plastered with sheets torn from a Bible, with the words 'God help me I have been cursed' scrawled in felt-tip pen. He had also received threatening telephone calls, and had been sent a cow's heart stuck with nails and a fetish doll wound with human hair. A farmer just outside Lewes found what appeared to be a black mass site set up in one of his barns, with an altar, burnt candles, incense, a photograph of Gargani and a note stating, 'I, Nicholas Gargani, renounce Christianity'.

Had poor Nicholas really been driven to his death by satanic curses? (He had apparently been cursed by two occultists in a Brighton pub, The Pig in Paradise). Was he being blackmailed ? He had withdrawn a substantial amount of money from his account, and has been trying to set up a loan for more. Or, according to the more febrile conspiracy theorists, had he been murdered for unspecified political reasons by a sinister brotherhood of high-ranking Sussex police officers because he Knew Too Much? And had they then planted evidence to implicate mysterious, uncatchable Satanists?

Some vociferous yet anonymous agitators believed that the Sussex police force itself was riddled with institutional Satanism, although they only managed to find one, a secretary in the Lewes Police Intelligence Department. She had been outed by the press in 1990 as having a penchant for sado-masochistic sex with men she liked to call Master, and found her kicks with a sinister sect based in Alfriston. Completely baseless rumours claimed that two police officers belonged to this group, which has now completely evaporated from the scene.

Nothing to help Nick or his family ever came of all this heated conjecture. The only plausible suspect for either murder or blackmail was Alex Smith, a 17-year-old supporter of both the BNP and the darkside, who had met Nicholas in 1995 and who had no alibi for the time of death. He came to the inquest to testify that Nicholas had been cursed, and that he had advised him to burn the cow's heart. Some not-very-reliable witnesses claimed that they were told by lower-ranking police officers at the inquest that they had been ordered to downplay any evidence that pointed to murder. The handwriting on the walls of Gargani's room was not his, according to his sister, but this was never forensically challenged. His keys, which he told friends had been missing for some days, turned up outside his front door just after his death. You don't need to invoke satanic powers to realise that someone could easily have got in and dressed the room with misleading biblical paperwork; nor would it be difficult to fake the remains of a black mass in a remote barn. To date, this is a tragic mystery that has never been solved.

More Salacious Detail

◗ *The Bishop of Monmouth, Dominic Walker, told the* Observer, *no less, that the satanic part of the sad story was probably the doing of a local quasi-satanic group called the Fellowship of Set, by which he probably meant the Temple of Set. The Temple of Set claimed right back that they were committed to non-violence and it was nothing to do with them*

PART FIVE

CADS & BOUNDERS

I have included this final chapter to give a home to those artful Sussex dodgers who got away with it, or almost did. People who rigged the system, who lived their lives on the premise that society's rules and customs did not apply to them because they were too posh, too smart, or too 'mad'. How else was I going to fit in the magnificent Aleister Crowley, the Great Beast of Hastings, far too entertaining a character to leave out, yet somehow not a natural fit for the Hanky Panky section? Or the murderers (alleged!) who evaded retribution by disappearing or by having friends in high places? And what about the con man who fleeced the mighty, and yet does not really mesh into the Chicanery section, or the dubious yet heroic revolutionary intent on regime destabilisation? As a group they may be disparate, but their unifying characteristic is that they are, in the immortal words of Terry-Thomas, 'an absolute shower'; but they are a Sussex shower, so we should be proud.

SAY YOU WANT A REVOLUTION

JACK CADE

'The first thing we do, let's kill all the lawyers!'

WILLIAM SHAKESPEARE, *HENRY VI PART II, ACT IV, SCENE II*

Whether you think Jack Cade was a hero or villain depends on your point of view, but almost a century and a half after his death, he was still notorious enough to land a supporting role in a Shakespeare play. And no, he wasn't really a Sussex boy, although he may have spent some time in the county: in fact no one knows where he came from, when he was born, or if his name was even Jack Cade – but he met his death on Sussex soil. On July 12th 1450 he was found mortally wounded at the hands of the Sheriff of Kent, Alexander Iden, just outside Heathfield; he died on the way to London, where his body was hung, drawn and quartered, just to make sure, and his head was cut off and displayed on London Bridge.

He may have been an Irishman called John Mortimer; he may have been a cousin of Richard, Duke of York (whose family name was Mortimer and who was an enemy of Henry VI); he may have been married to a wealthy Kentish woman and been living under the name of John Aylmer or Aylmere; he certainly fought as a soldier in France. Whoever he was, Cade had charisma by the wagon load – he came from virtually nowhere and moulded disparate groups of men from Kent and Sussex into a fighting force of around 20,000 that actually defeated the King's army at the Battle (downgraded to skirmish by some sniffy historians) of Sevenoaks on June 18th 1450.

The rebellion had the backing of much of the populace. Henry VI was an unpopular monarch. The bribery and corruption in his court, the indiscriminate land-grabbing and the swingeing taxes Henry levied to pay for the interminable Hundred Years War (which actually overran to 116 years) rallied most people to the cause. It wasn't a rabble of raggle-taggle disorganised peasants: they were tradesmen, craftsmen, landowners, civil servants and even some clergy. Sussex worthies who joined Cade included the rector of Mayfield, the prior of St Pancras in Lewes, and some men from Fletching, including one Peter Denot, the village glover.

Cade and the revolutionary army (by now around 46,000 strong) crossed Deptford Bridge into London on July 3rd. They engineered the beheading of the King's unpopular treasurer, Lord Saye and Sele (Sir James Fiennes) and the equally unpopular Sheriff of Kent, William Cromer (both readily expendable; Lord Saye was already in the tower on an impeachment charge). A truce was called, and Cade presented a long list of demands, including the return of Richard, Duke of York (a Mortimer, remember) and pardons for the rebels. A deal was brokered and most of the rebels went home.

Many were later killed in suspicious circumstances, including Cade himself. After they had supposedly achieved their aims, he and his followers, including many liberated from Southwark gaol, allegedly went on the plundering rampage and lost popular support. They squabbled their way back to Rochester where apparently Cade fell out with his followers over the distribution of booty. On July 10th a procla-mation was issued against him in the name of Cade (he had been pardoned under the name of Mortimer) and a price put on his head. He fled to Sussex, closely followed by the new Sheriff of Kent, Alexander Iden, who hunted him down and was rewarded with a smart castle.

It is theoretically possible that Jack Cade was killed at Hothfield near Ashford, Kent, and that Cade Street in East Sussex was named in error, but this is almost certainly a rumour spread by jealous Kentish natives.

More Salacious Detail

◎ A roadside monument stands just north of the Battle road, Cade Street, announcing that Jack Cade, rebel, was killed here by Alexander Iden, Sheriff of Kent

◎ You can still see the gateway and the outlines of the moat at the Sheriff of Kent's castle at Iden

THE GREAT BEAST OF HASTINGS

ALEISTER CROWLEY 1875-1947

'And I rave; and I rape and I rip and I rend Everlasting, world without end,
Mannikin, maiden, Maenad, man, In the might of Pan.'

ALEISTER CROWLEY, *HYMN TO PAN*

On December 1st 1947, a sudden gust of wind and a solitary thunderclap disturbed an otherwise quiet day in Sussex, coinciding with the death of Aleister Crowley, the Great Beast 666 and the Wickedest Man in the World. Or so the story goes. However, like much of the mythology surrounding the occult philosopher and writer, the truth is a bit more prosaic – but no less fascinating. Crowley spent his final years in Hastings, after a lifetime devoted to hedonistic indulgence in occult practices involving sexual promiscuity ('sex magick'), habitual drug-taking and even human sacrifice. Allegedly. But Sussex people – and Hastonians in particular – are not easily shocked, and his arrival in the town caused hardly a ripple. In fact he fitted in rather well with his eccentric and bohemian adopted home, and we can only wonder why it took him so long to find it.

Disappointingly, most of Crowley's salacious life was spent outside Sussex, but he did manage one posthumous scandal here. At his very sparsely attended funeral in Brighton, his friend Louis Wilkinson read Crowley's priapic poem *Hymn to Pan*. This so scandalised Brighton residents that they demanded the council make sure this sort of 'black mass' never be allowed to take place again.

The young Beast

He was born Edward Alexander Crowley (he assumed the name Aleister, which he disliked, for poetic and magical reasons, but mainly because he hated being called 'Alick') in 1875 at Leamington Spa, into a family of Exclusive Brethren, a fundamentalist branch of the Plymouth Brethren. Even in prudish Victorian society, they stood out as a stiflingly puritanical sect. Basically, what they believed was that if it was enjoyable, it must be sinful. As a child, if Aleister showed any signs of rebellion against this strict code, his mother called him 'The Beast'. You can see where this is leading, can't you? Crowley Snr made a small fortune from the family brewing firm (he apparently didn't mind profiting from other people's sins). This paid for young Crowley to attend public school, including a period at Eastbourne College, and then to study at Trinity College, Cambridge, where, unsurprisingly, he finally broke from his religious upbringing, discovered his (initially homosexual) libido and began his researches into mysticism and the occult. He had other interests, notably chess and mountaineering, at which he was rather good, but they were a bit too wholesome for the diabolic persona he seemed anxious to cultivate. He embarked on an exploration of the sex life previously denied him. In the all-male environment of Trinity College, however, this meant either picking up prostitutes or homosexual liaisons: equal opportunist Crowley opted for both. His poetry also helped to bolster the 'wicked' image, starting with a collection of 'shocking' pornographic verse under the less-than-subtle title *White Stains*.

Sex magick

In 1899, after a short period living in London as Count Vladimir Svareff, Crowley bought the forbidding Boleskine House on the shores of Loch Ness, where he liked to be known as the Laird of Boleskine and Abertarff. Immediately, rumours began to circulate that his occult experiments had caused the murderous insanity of a lodgekeeper, the local butcher to cut off his own fingers, and worse. In 1903, after time out for a safari break in India and some 'sex magick' research in Paris, he met a young widow, Rose Kelly, who complained of a stream of admirers wanting her hand in marriage. Crowley proposed a platonic marriage of convenience, and they married the next day – but his promise of non-consummation was promptly broken.

Rose's mental health was already fragile, but marriage to Crowley proved the last straw. She took to drink, and was eventually committed to an asylum, but not before providing him with a revelation that was to change the course of his life. On their honeymoon in Egypt, Rose started behaving even more oddly than usual, which Crowley interpreted as some kind of possession by the god Horus. In the guise of Aiwass, minister of Horus, she nominated him as a prophet and dictated *The Book of the Law*, which formed the basis of his subsequent magical activities, and whose basic message was 'Do what thou wilt' (a dictum he happily adopted as his motto). He began composing the *Holy Books of Thelema*, (*thelema* is Greek for will or intention) and founded his own magical society, The Silver Star, which performed the mysterious Rites of Eleusis in Caxton Hall in 1910 to a gratifyingly outraged public. By this time, he had divorced Rose, as she had outlived her usefulness, and had a string of lovers to perform his sex-magick – probably cultivated to provide him with an income, as he had worked his way through his father's fortune: it is said that he soon tired of the women, and the men soon tired of him.

In 1913, he sold Bolsekine House and spent the war years in America, either as an anti-British Irishman and German propaganda agent, or working for British counterintelligence, depending on who you believe. In peacetime, however, he soon reverted to the role he enjoyed most, settling in Cefalù, Sicily with his pregnant lover Leah Hirsig and establishing the Abbey of Thelema to get on with the sex magick. Tales of a disciple dying after drinking the blood of sacrificed cats, promiscuity and drug-taking didn't go down too well with *i Fascisti*, and Crowley was chucked out of Italy. And then out of France, amid rumours of human sacrifice.

The Wickedest Man in the World?

Back in Britain, he continued to scandalise. In 1934 he sued the artist Nina Hamnett (aka the Queen of Bohemia, and colleague of Bloomsbury groupie Roger Fry) for referring to him as a black magician in her book *The Laughing Torso* (1932). The high-profile court case, which he lost, bankrupted him, but secured his reputation as the Wickedest Man in the World. Mr Justice Swift obligingly summed up by saying: 'I have never heard such dreadful, horrible, blasphemous and abominable stuff as that which has been produced by the man (Crowley) who describes himself to you as the greatest living poet'.

By the end of World War II, Crowley was an old man, addicted to heroin (prescribed for asthma and bronchitis), no longer capable of vigorous sex magick, and broke. Louis Wilkinson suggested he take a room in an eccentric guesthouse in Hastings, run by the bohemian Kathleen 'Johnny' Symonds and her husband Vernon. And so, in late 1945, a telegram arrived at Netherwood, The Ridge, telling the owners to expect a consignment of frozen meat. The GPO had alerted the Ministry of Food, whose inspectors were waiting when an ambulance delivered a grinning Crowley.

He spent the last two years of his life at Netherwood, teaching the landlady's son Latin, beating all comers at the local chess club, walking around the town and keeping himself to himself in his room (No. 13, of course). There are several myths concerning his death, including the apocryphal last words 'I am perplexed' or in an alternative version, 'Sometimes I hate myself', and the report of a sudden thunderclap; more probable is the story that he just collapsed in his room, and was found dead by a cleaner who heard the crash as he fell. Residents of Hastings insist he put a curse on the town, condemning them to never be able to escape from it without taking a pebble from the beach (or a stone from the town wall), but as he seemed to quite like the place and fitted in well with its offbeat atmosphere, this seems unlikely.

Crowley loved being outrageous, especially to shock those who didn't share his intelligence, education or sense of humour. And, although he did get up to all sorts of things that were frowned upon by polite society, and treated women abominably, there's little foundation for the rumours of satanic human sacrifice and evil magic: not so much the spawn of Beelzebub, more a very naughty boy.

More Salacious Detail

⊙ *Netherwood was demolished in the 1970s to make way for a housing estate. Crowley fans talk of a meeting of ley lines and a mysterious aura about the area, but this is not apparent in the rather anonymous suburbia there today*

⊙ *Boleskine House once belonged to Led Zeppelin's Jimmy Page. Led Zeppelin also bought Hammerwood Park, East Grinstead, but forgot all about it*

⊙ *François Rabelais, the renaissance prankster who Crowley would surely have read, invented the Abbey of Thelema in* Gargantua and Pantagruel *(1532)*

OMERTÀ IN UCKFIELD

LUCKY LORD LUCAN

'I have had a traumatic night of unbelievable coincidences.'

LETTER FROM RICHARD JOHN BINGHAM, 7TH EARL OF LUCAN TO MICHAEL STOOP,
7 NOVEMBER 1974

Even though he has not been verifiably seen for 35 years, Richard John Bingham, 7th Earl of Lucan, remains fascinating. 'Lucky' Lucan spotting is still a popular sport and sightings have been reported from all over the world, particularly the USA, Canada, Africa, and South America, the traditional refuge of European badboys.

So what claim has Sussex on the errant earl? Well, the last time he was officially seen was in Uckfield, of all places, and the car he was driving, a Ford Corsair borrowed from a friend, was discovered abandoned and suspiciously full of clues, in Newhaven, not far from the ferry terminal. Although the crime of which he was accused was not committed on Sussex soil, his mysterious and dramatic disappearance is all ours.

At an inquest held on June 5th 1975, the jury took 31 minutes to name Lord Lucan guilty of murdering his children's nanny, Sandra Rivett. Months previously, on November 7th 1974, some time before 9 pm, Lord Lucan had let himself into the home of his estranged wife at 46 Lower Belgrave Street, London. He knew it was the nanny's night off; he knew his wife always came downstairs to the basement kitchen to make herself a pot of tea at 9 o'clock. He took the lightbulb out of its socket and waited in the dark with a length of lead piping. So far, so Cluedo; when a woman came into the kitchen carrying a tray of tea things, he pounced and bludgeoned her to death. Unfortunately, when he looked closer he found that it was poor Sandra Rivett dead on the floor in a pool of blood, not Lady Lucan. He panicked and stuffed the body into the sack he had brought along for the purpose, but was then disturbed by the real Lady Lucan, whom he attacked. She fought back, and managed to get out and raise the alarm at the local pub, The Plumbers Arms.

By the time police had arrived, Lord Lucan had gone. He had driven to Uckfield, to the house of his friends Ian and Susan Maxwell Scott.

He told Mrs Maxwell Scott that he happened to be walking past his old home when he saw someone attacking Lady Lucan. Naturally he rushed in to save the day, getting covered in blood in the process, but then discovered that it was the nanny who was dead, not his wife. However, he did not want to call the police as he believed that his wife would jump at the chance to accuse him of murder because she hated him so much. Despite all the advantages of education and background, Lucan had decided that professional gambling was the career for him; consequently he was in deep financial trouble and facing bankruptcy. His marriage had broken down. He had tried to get custody of his children, but failed; a murder charge would not improve his chances. Mrs Maxwell Scott apparently believed him but could not stop him driving off into the night. Three days later his empty car was discovered in Newhaven. Of Lord L. there was nothing.

A few honest souls believe that his story was true and that he was so ashamed of the impending bankruptcy and scandal that he did the decent thing and threw himself off the night ferry to France. A few more believe that he had hired a hitman to kill his wife, but arranged to clear away the body himself (hence the sack and the borrowed car) because he was on a budget. And that then he did the decent thing, etc. But most people believe that he is alive and well, unless age has taken him, safe in a cocoon spun by the Old Boy Network of the rich and privileged. The hot money is on Lucky being smuggled to France by his gambling buddies John Aspinall and Sir James Goldsmith. Both are dead now, and both went to their graves with their lips sealed; as did Susan Maxwell Scott. We will never know for sure.

More Salacious Detail

❯ Go to www.lordlucan.com for the latest news on Lucan sightings

❯ Lord Lucan's ancestor, George Bingham, the 3rd Earl of Lucan, was the man who sent the Light Brigade into the valley of death at the Battle of Balaclava in 1854

THE SQUIRE OF GRAFFHAM

GARTON ORME & THE CURSED WILLOW

'Oh, Willow Willow Waley!'

TRADITIONAL FOLKSONG

In the early 18th century, the village of Graffham, near Petworth, was a bit like a Wild West fiefdom. It was owned and run by a squirearchy. This is all very well when the incumbent is rubicund and benevolent like Fielding's Squire Weston, but when they're mean and murderous, you can see why democracy rules.

Graffham had been in the clutches of the Orme family since 1675, when William Garton, the last of the male line of Gartons died and left it to his sister Mary and her husband Robert Orme; in 1578, the manor had been presented by the Earl of Arundel to Giles Garton, a London ironmonger, so the Garton Ormes had no reason to puff themselves up. Bear with me, I am just setting the scene.

According to boring old records, Squire Orme married Charlotte Hanway in 1715 when he was only 20. However, village tradition is much more exciting and has it different. This version claims that he was married before this to an anonymous and, it has to be said, rather nebulous young woman, whom he walled up until she was dead, because he could. Allegedly she could not bear children, although he did not give her much time; neither did she approve of his reckless addiction to the gamin' tables to which Georgian gentlemen were so attracted. He hung around with the better-looking village wenches, one in particular (although why he could not have just exercised *droit de seigneur* is a bit beyond me) while the villagers wondered where his lady had got to. There was eventually a funeral, with a coffin and everything, which was interred in the family vault near the altar in the village church, but the villagers who, being Sussex people, would not be druv, insisted that the poor emaciated body of his wife had been thrown down the well to hide the evidence. Many people saw her ghost. The squire sloped off to lay low for a bit (and once again, the timing is a bit elastic here) then returned, but made the cardinal mistake of not marrying the girl he had supposedly killed for, but going for the more respectable option of Charlotte the rector's daughter (as per the records).

Despite marriage into the clergy, the squire did not reform. The original Wench became pregnant; Orme would have nothing to do with her and so her father took the folkloric route, went to the village pond in the middle of the night and cursed Squire Orme under the boughs of the weeping willow. Willows, as all country folk know, are one of the nine sacred trees of Wicca, belong to the goddess of the moon in all her phases, and are firmly on the side of the feminine principle. They are also the symbol of forsaken love. Do not mess with willows. The father's curse was that there should be no male heir born at Graffham, a fearsome thing in the time of male primogeniture. Sure enough, wicked Squire Orme only produced one daughter (that he knew about) in 1723, then died in 1758. It was a very slow curse. But it seemed to work, as Orme's daughter had only a daughter and eventually the manor passed to far-flung reaches of male relatives by marriage, because everybody produced daughters, or sons who were not very good at surviving.

So far, so Stella Gibbons, but some rational reinforcements were on the way. In 1833, Bishop Samuel Wilberforce, Soapy Sam, the preacher who took on Darwin in the apes and angels furore, married into the family and became the lord of the manor. His rector, also his brother-in-law, was Henry Manning (later Cardinal Manning). During some routine work in the church, the coffin (remember that?) was dug up. Manning thought it excessively heavy, and had it opened to reveal... that it was full of stones! The villagers felt vindicated and there was much talk of the curse until Wilberforce's son, Reginald, finally burnt down the offending willow to stop all that kind of nonsense. However, male heirs are still few and far between at Graffham. Nice to think of women getting their own back.

More Salacious Detail

◉ Garton Orme at the Spinet *is a portrait of the pre-murderous 12-year-old Squire Orme of Graffham looking angelic and playing the spinet in his lovely blue frock coat, painted in 1707 by Jonathan Richardson the Elder. You can see it in the Holburne Museum in Bath*

OLD NICK IN NEWICK

THE HUSTLER'S TALE

*'Make the lie big, make it simple, keep saying it,
and eventually they will believe it.'*

ADOLF HITLER

This is a heartwarming tale of the audacious fleecing of the rich and holy of Newick by a bold-faced pilfering fence at the top of his game. You would not believe this happened in the 1980s; it reads like something Chaucer would have been proud of. Imagine it. *A conne-man ther was of Leedes towne, y-wis...* It's not as if he were dealing with an easily-led pitchfork-waving mob; anyone can control one of those. He went for the gentry (Viscounts Brentford and Hampden, the Earl of March, who owned Goodwood Racecourse and should, you feel, have been a finer judge of horse-flesh), the pillar of society (magistrate and later High Sheriff Michael Warren), the cloth (the Reverend John Baker, Rector of Newick) and the rich grocer's wife (Mrs Susan Sainsbury). And he fleeced them all, although not as thoroughly as a hedge fund manager might have done.

When Derry Mainwaring Knight (and if you are going to take an assumed name, make it one with knobs on) came out of his Hull gaol in 1983 after serving time for rape, he emerged into a society in the thrall of Satanic Ritual Abuse mania, a kind of communal moral panic that swept certain sections of society. It was a gift. How is someone with form to live? On his wits, that's how. You have to admire DMK in a kind of rabbit-in-the-headlights way. Not for him the small-time cons and desperate pyramid selling. He came up with a genius plan. Almost without a pause, he leapt aboard the satanic bandwagon and by February 1984 had smarmed his way into the trust of John Baker the rector of the affluent village of Newick (no point trying to grift off those who have nothing) and told him a truly flabbergasting tale. He had, he claimed, been baptised in human blood and dedicated to the Dark Lord by his evil grandmother at birth. He had seen the light and wanted to smash the satanic cult before it brought harm to even more innocents, but he had taken vows, he found it almost impossible to break free, the blood bond was so strong… and the Satanists were all ready to kill anyone who betrayed their secrets, especially a trusty like him… but if only two large debts could be paid off, and some more money be found so that he could buy up satanic regalia and instruments (he could lay his hands on them as a member of the cult) and destroy them for ever, he would be a free soul and the world would be rid of one more satanic tentacle. Who could say no? (If you're going to lie make it a big one.) Knight worked hard for the money, praying nightly with the rector and falling into trances and becoming the mouthpiece for the Dark One whenever things got a bit sticky. ('You cannot have him. He belongs to Lucifer.') Between February and May the following year, the rector managed to raise around £216,000 from his wealthy parishioners (*see above*) and gave it all to Knight, who spent it on fast cars and faster women and financing his lucrative sidelines (drugs and prostitution).

It all went wrong of course. Satanic Ritual Abuse was no longer flavour of the month and accountants stepped in. Knight went before Judge Neil Dennison at Maidstone, for a sensational nine-week trial for which every redtop in the land was truly thankful. He still tried to play the demon card, claiming that his satanic cult had ordered him to plead guilty so that the trial could end and their secrets would remain secret, but he had resisted for the greater good. It didn't work, mainly because he also cheerily boasted of never having come across anyone whom he couldn't part from their money. He was found guilty on 19 charges of obtaining money and property by deception, gaoled for seven years and fined £50,000. Of course the trial cost the taxpayer four times the amount that Knight had screwed out of the Newick set, but that just shows you whose side lawyers are on.

More Salacious Detail

◎ *The Reverend Baker was, it has been said, a keen conjurer, known as Presto John when he was whipping rabbits out of hats, and a member of the International Brotherhood of Magicians. Makes you think, doesn't it?*

THE ANGEL OF EASTBOURNE

JOHN BODKIN ADAMS 1899-1983

'She wanted to die — that cannot be murder...
It is impossible to accuse a doctor.'

JOHN BODKIN ADAMS

Half a century before Dr Harold Shipman, Sussex had its own angel of death in the portly figure of Eastbourne's Dr John Bodkin Adams. When he was arrested on December 19th 1956 on suspicion of murdering 81-year-old Edith Morrell by morphine injection six years previously, he was the wealthiest doctor in England. Despite being brought up amid the fundamentalist austerity of the Plymouth Brethren, he had no qualms about luxurious living. He was beneficiary of more than 132 wills, raking in over £45,000 in cash, plus jewellery, shares, silver, antiques and luxury motors. And there are countless witness accounts of his walking off with little, and sometimes quite large, expensive items from his patients' houses, while they were still warm under the morphine cosh he had administered.

His medical skills were indifferent. As an anaesthetist he frequently chomped on cakes or fell asleep at his post during operations and either cyanosed his patients or underdosed them so they woke up mid surgery. No other doctors in Eastbourne wanted to work with him. Elderly patients wilted and faded away after a short time under his care. Gossip sloshed and eddied through the tearooms and hotel lounges, yet he prospered. Either he was the most cack-handed physician the world had ever seen, but possessed an irresistible bedside manner; or he was a merciful mercenary, selling easeful death to wealthy patients; or he was a cold-hearted killer who murdered the helpless because he had the means and they had the money. You choose.

The case against

Superintendent Herbert Hannam of Scotland Yard suspected that Adams had despatched at least 163 people before their time, and had painstakingly built up a damning case against him based on two deaths, those of

Edith Morrell (1950) and Gertrude Hullett (1956). Yet on April 15th 1957, after 17 days at the Old Bailey (the longest murder trial Britain had seen to date), Adams was acquitted; the jury took under an hour to find him not guilty. What had gone wrong?

It's hard now not to conclude that the Establishment closed ranks and nobbled the trial. While there is no evidence that Adams was black-mailing anybody, he was in possession of knowledge which, if made public, would have been extremely embarrassing to those in high places.

The prosecution appeared to sabotage its own case. Vital evidence was lost or destroyed while in police hands. The DPP had, bafflingly, made the major charge the murder of Edith Morrell; her body had been cremated almost as instantly as she had died, destroying any evidence, Adams having signed the cremation consent form, illegally. The Attorney General, Sir Reginald Manningham Buller, leading for the prosecution, put on a great show of bullying, yet allowed opposing counsel first shot at the nurses' notes, which they built into a very strong defence. The British Medical Association leant on their Eastbourne members, only two of whom gave evidence. Adams himself was not called to the stand.

A political decision

That Adams had some sort of hold over the Eastbourne aristocracy became apparent. Sir Roland Gwynne, magistrate and mayor of Eastbourne, was Adams's friend and patient; he visited him daily at 9 o'clock in the morning and they went on holidays together. Gwynne's brother was Rupert Gwynne, one-time MP for Eastbourne. This gave Adams a connection to Edward Cavendish, the 10th Duke of Devonshire, whose physician he became. The Duke died in Adams's care on November 26th 1950, two weeks after Edith Morrell.

The Duke's sister was married to Harold Macmillan, who had taken over as Prime Minister in January 1957 at the helm of a very tottery post-Suez government. And Lady Macmillan had been having an affair with Robert Boothby MP for the previous 20 years; perhaps it was feared that if this somehow became public knowledge, via the Adams trial, the government could fall.

Dirty work becomes more plausible when you know that Manningham Buller was distantly related to the Devonshires and that he regularly attended cabinet meetings. Nothing has ever been proved, nor will be, but it is very likely that the 163 people who died in extremely suspicious circumstances, and the poor old Duke himself, allegedly, were the collateral damage of a pragmatic political decision.

There was a sop to justice, although not a very juicy one. Adams was later found guilty at Lewes Assizes of 13 counts of forging prescriptions, falsifying death certificates, obstructing a police search and failing to keep a dangerous drugs register. He was fined £2,400 – no kind of punishment at all for a man of his wealth and means – and struck off the medical register. Four years later he was quietly reinstated and practised in Eastbourne until his death in 1983, although he was banned for life from prescribing dangerous drugs. A bit late, really.

<hr/>

More Salacious Detail

❯ *Apparently Adams loaned the Rolls-Royce Silver Dawn that Gertrude Hullett bequeathed him to the Eastbourne Carnival Committee as a coach for the carnival queen*

INDEX